Whitewash

Rhys Christian

Copyright © 2014 Rhys Christian

The characters and events portrayed in this book are entirely fictitious. Any resemblance to actual persons, living or dead, is entirely coincidental.

No part of this publication may be reproduced, distributed, or transmitted in any form or by any means, including photocopying, recording, or other electronic or mechanical methods, without the prior written permission of the publisher.

Rhys Christian asserts the moral right to be identified as the author of this work.

Published by London Backstreet Press.

All rights reserved.

ISBN-13: 978-1505663433
ISBN-10: 1505663431

For Reece

1. Ireland (1970's)

Saturday am. County Laois.

A metalled road emerges from mist that hides the left horizon. It cuts a causeway over flat bog that fills the scene, disappears into mist that hides the right horizon.

Beside the road three men bent, cutting peat. Two more men yards off. These last two carry carbines slung over their shoulders. The party wear regulation oilskins.

Out of the mist a silent headlight. Slowly then steadily brighter. The sound of its approach carried off in the rain. One of the diggers spots it, puts down his cutter, stands up. The two others straighten and follow his gaze.

The rider sees the men as he is upon them. He skids to a halt, opens the visor of his full face helmet and yells at the party.

No response.

Rider signals to guards with bike mitts, indicates side box of motorbike.

[Red lettering- "ZZ DISPATCH - LIMERICK" is written across side box over yellow and white symbol of a lightning bolt. As rider bends down same insignia can be seen sown into the back of his leather jacket.]

Guards unshoulder weapons.

Rider pulls paper package from side box, holds it high in mittened hand.

First guard motions with carbine for rider to come

down to where he is standing.

Rider leaves engine idling, props bike on side stand and dismounts. Jumps down from road onto peat ground. His visor drops shut.

Rider Delivery for the Governor.

Guard nods, says nothing.

Rider Is this the right road?

Guard looks into rider's visor, sees only his own blurred reflection.

Rider Can you hear me?

Rider tenders package for guard to inspect. Guard looks at package, reads what is written on it. He looks at insignia on motorbike side box.

Guard From Limerick?

Rider Yes.

Guard You're English.

Rider raises both mittens towards guard in a gesture of innocence.

Rider Strange, yeah?

Point blank. Rider fires through mitten into guard's face.

One of diggers, who has manoeuvred himself to within two yards, brings peat cutter down on to second guard's skull. Second guard falls to ground. Prisoner drives angled blade into his face.

Rider turns to two other prisoners.

Rider Boys... Your worries are over... Rest in peace.

Rider executes both men, taking each with a single shot between the eyes. He jumps back up to road, remounts bike, kicks away side stand.

...We're outa here!

Pulls off shredded mitten to reveal snub nosed revolver taped into palm of inner leather glove. Tape and glove scorched black. Begins unwinding tape.

Prisoner [giving an order] The gun... This one's got it coming.

Rider There's no time for this.

Prisoner There's always time for this...

Prisoner catches lobbed revolver, kneels over second guard who is already clearly dead. Empties three remaining chambers into hole in man's face.

... Fat bastard!

Prisoner scrambles up to road, hands revolver to rider, jumps pillion onto bike.

Rider opens cylinder of revolver, ejects spent brass onto road. Takes speed loader from jacket, refills chambers then pockets revolver before engaging gear.

Motorbike turns, heads west for the hidden horizon. Somewhere, before its tail light is lost in mist, it seems to stop, as if at a crossroads. For a few seconds it does not move, then it changes direction and is gone.

ACT 1

2. Harley Street, Central London.

Monday pm. The first floor salon of a period house. The consulting room of a society doctor.

French windows open onto a balcony that overlooks a busy street. Inside these windows a leather chaise-longue. In the centre of the room three leather armchairs arranged in front of an antique mahogany desk. This desk spread with papers and copies of medical journals. A number of prints of X-rays seem to be the subject of a half written letter on monogrammed writing paper. A quill pen has been left lying on a blotting pad.

Between the desk and the back windows of the room, which have full length venetian blinds, now open, is a screen. A man stands just inside the screened off area. He is six foot tall and of heavy build. Too well fed without being fat he otherwise cuts a figure of some distinction, though at the moment he seems a little red faced. The man is about sixty years old. He is wearing a charcoal grey business suit that has a broad pinstripe; a bow tie over a striped business shirt. He has on a pair of half moon spectacles and he is looking at an extraordinary sight.

An exotic, yet somewhat dishevelled woman is lying flat on her back on an examination couch. The woman is probably between thirty five and forty. She is fully clothed, in a manner of speaking. Over her bare skin she has a leather waistcoat that is several sizes too small and which does not reach as far down as her belly button. Her breasts are threatening to burst the only popper that is still fastened. Her hips are circled by a leather belt that has a bronze buckle in the design of a snake's head. Beneath the belt her small belly has burst the waist button of her leather trousers and the zip has undone itself far enough to reveal red pubic hairs, which may be glistening with sweat, creeping over the elastic of a scrap of thin white cotton. The woman's legs are encased in black leather boots, knee high. The spiked heels of the boots have torn the paper blanket that she lies on and they threaten to pierce the plastic covered mattress beneath.

Her pale skin looks as though it would be soft to the touch. Her skull, lying back on its shredded pillow of red hair looks fragile. Her freckled face, which has no make-up, seems kind, if sad. The wreck of an Amazon.

The man looks up from the woman's body, through the window towards an office block behind the house. There, a man and a woman are standing at a high window discussing the contents of a sheet of paper.

The woman on the couch reeks of alcohol. Her shiny handbag, unzipped on an instrument table beside her head, has an open bottle of Johnny Walker poking out of it. In her right hand a fat and badly rolled joint. In her left hand the stem of a mangled rose, trophy of a recently concluded encounter. She speaks deliberately but lucidly, and in the definitive nasal tones of the English upper class, while drawing shapes in the air around her head with the joint.

Woman So good of you to see me, Doctor... and at such short notice.

Man Are you sick today?

Woman Sick of you wasting my time. Is it here?

Man You are wasting your time if you think it's here.

Woman Where then?

Man Somewhere safe.

Woman You did steal it?... Why, oh why, deny it for so long?

Man All things in good time.

Woman You can get it?

Man When the time is right.

PAUSE

Woman You're in too deep to deal.

Man I'm in too deep not to deal. You got me in too deep.

Woman This can be over.

Man The photos. And all the negatives. Slabb gets the report on the Secretary.

Woman Play it straight, why don't you?

Man When you don't? *[pause]* If you would we could see our way out of this.

Woman *[laughs sleepily]* You want to fuck me?

Man Doesn't every man?

Woman Don't force me to brag. So vulgar.

Man Already had a man today?... How many? Shall we say in the last twenty four hours?

Woman *[theatrically checks her watch and shrugs]* Like I say, wouldn't want to brag.

Man You lovely bitch.

The man stands over the woman, slips his hand inside her unzipped trousers and begins to finger her. The woman closes her eyes.

The man hesitates. In the office block that overlooks people seem to be gathering at windows. He takes his hand from her panties, goes to the windows and begins turning down the blinds.

Woman[*laughing*] Chicken.

The man closes all the blinds and fastens them. He turns back to find the woman asleep and snoring.

3. White City

Monday. Hot afternoon. Tenements and towers, idols in a thick haze that sits over the urban desert. A body thrown from a high window might yet be carried safe to ground.

Somewhere, at the feet of concrete towers, a small brick built block of flats has a flagstone courtyard that is surrounded by cast iron railings painted a bright blue. The same blue railings line the stairways and walkways of the block. The flats all have leaded windows. Cherry trees inhabit the courtyard.

Here it is strangely quiet, sane even, somehow insulated against the waters of madness that flow beyond the blue railings. This old block, built by charity to house the hopeless and the fallen, has now taken on an air of desirability, if not respectability, amid its surroundings. Families wait years for a flat to 'come up.'

The flat we are in is in a prime position in the block. A corner flat on the top, third, floor. The kitchen of the flat is a small room, about twelve feet by eight, but it is well lit with a pleasant double aspect. Through one of these windows the branches of one of the cherry trees can be seen, near enough to knock on the glass on a windy night. By day, as now, small and not so small birds land and take off in rotation. Three people are seated at the kitchen table.

Slabb. *A man of about fifty, by appearance a labourer. Hands and fingers that could crush an apple to juice. Small blue eyes in a big face that once might have been handsome in a brutish way.*

Cathleen. *A tired looking woman of similar age. A faded beauty. Straggly black hair. Green eyes ringed* *black. Pale rouged cheeks. She is braless in a very low cut tee shirt that has the word 'Yes' printed as a support to her mottled cleavage. A dumpy rag doll with bruised arms.*

Weed. *A thin sick man. Heavy lensed glasses give him stary eyes in a bony head. Delicate hands. Nicotine stained fingers. He has the shakes.*

Slabb Sunday night he's here. Six days, fuck sake, and we're history... When did we let them down?

Cathleen I thought it was just a rumour put out. You know, the bogeyman's coming.

Slabb Some rumour. They sprung him Saturday and he killed four men. For fun, as I heard it. Now he's coming our way and they're laying the red carpet.

Cathleen I heard he'd gone soft. Inside.

Slabb Who told you that?

Cathleen In the head I mean. Gone funny.

Slabb Depends on your sense of humour. Myself, I don't find Donal Brady funny. But that's only me, maybe others do. Yourself for instance. We all know...

Cathleen Know what, exactly?

Slabb You and him were like that. He was your first, wasn't he?

Weed *(interjects, giggling)* First of a very long line.

Cathleen You hold your tongue.

Slabb Never forgotten him? Well, you can kiss it but I'm not. Why should I? I built all this up nice. By myself. And for the both of us by the way. Look at the take in The Crypt. Didn't I do that? Didn't I get rid of the competition?

Weed And didn't I help?

Slabb looks at Weed as if he were an insect.

Slabb You scared them shitless.

Cathleen He's been a help to you.

Slabb No one better with pencil and paper. Just don't ask him to use a pencil sharpener. Might cut his own throat.

PAUSE... the three look at each other as if this is yet another beginning of the argument that has been heard weekly, if not nightly, over the past...

Weed Sunday night.

Cathleen No time to get ready.

Slabb You've a lot to do. Lose a couple of pounds, new hairstyle, nail job, new outfits. How will you manage?

Cathleen You bastard.

Slabb You take this lying down. It's what you're good at... Not me.

Cathleen *[mocking]* And?

Slabb Someone's coming to help.

Cathleen Who someone?

Slabb Someone you don't know. Someone I don't know. Someone who can help us. Anyway, someone who can help us help ourselves.

Cathleen Do you intend making yourself plain at some point?

Slabb There's a man... Knows who we are, what we are. We're not just some paddies who dig the road.

Weed Knows what we do?

Slabb Yes.

Cathleen English?

Slabb Yes.

Cathleen And?

Slabb Lets us be...

Cathleen Police?

Slabb Sort of.

Cathleen Could put us out of business?

Slabb If he wanted.

Cathleen And into jail?

Slabb Certainly.

Weed Why doesn't he?

Slabb He's got his reasons.

Weed What are they?

Slabb I don't ask.

Weed You don't ask? When a man who could kill you is letting you live?

Slabb Do you look a gift horse in the mouth then?

Cathleen You're paying him.

Slabb does not reply to this... EXTENDED PAUSE.

Weed Jesus. They call us the terrorists. We're the only ones with any morals.

Slabb Is it moral what they're going to do to us? In six days?

Weed Forget it. How's this whoever he is going to help?

Slabb He's sending one of his men. Someone we can trust. *[turns to Cathleen]* You'll have to be nice to him.

Weed Christ, Michael. Can't anything happen without that?

Slabb She knows where her interests lie. We all do. Let's grow up.

PAUSE... Slabb and Weed both turn and look at Cathleen. She stares back at both of them. In turn both men avoid her eyes.

Weed This copper, what does he know?

Slabb What he has to.

Weed What do they say?

Slabb Keep him sweet. For now.

Weed For now?

Slabb For now.

Weed He doesn't know that.

Slabb He will do.

Weed They help?

Slabb Of course. What are we, big time?

Weed The Doc and Looby Loo?

Slabb He knows.

Weed Do they know that?

Slabb Yes.

Weed And?

Slabb The report. Nothing else matters.

Weed Which is why Brady?

Slabb Why Brady is what I say. I could handle it.

Weed Yeah?

Slabb Haven't I up to now?

Weed You haven't up to now. That's what this is about. They want it. Where is it?

Slabb It's her.

Weed But what are you doing about it?

Slabb Or it's The Doc. He's stalling.

Weed What are you doing either way?

Slabb I just said. This copper's sending a man.

Weed And they're sending Brady... I told you not to use that tramp. She's off her head.

Cathleen Could be she's not as far gone as she seems.

Weed Takes one to know one.

4. London Street, Paddington

Monday. Mid-afternoon. By the dead gardens. A smell of fried onions, stale beer and urine hangs in the street.

Trafalgar. *A mandarin from an unnamed Department.*

Quinn. *A sometime operative.*

Quinn and Trafalgar in the back of Trafalgar's staff saloon. The driver across the street 'on cigarette break'.

Trafalgar talking, Quinn listening. Through the side window both men watching a woman wino on a nearby bench. Red faced and laughing, and with her short skirt rucked around her waist, she is trying to drink from a can as two men either side of her fondle her thighs. She has good legs.

On the back seat between Quinn and Trafalgar a pile of tabloid newspapers. Their dates cover a period of several months- "JUNIOR MINISTER GOES- GOOD RIDDANCE WE SAY"-"NOT FIT FOR OFFICE, FO TOP DOG SENT PACKING"- "GOVERNED BY A BUNCH OF GAYS? NO THANKS".

On Trafalgar's lap, the front page of the broadsheet Daily Telegraph- 'STOLEN MEDICAL RECORDS MAY EMBARRASS CABINET MINISTER'. "A document that has gone missing from an as yet unnamed private clinic, but which is thought to be in south-west London and which may specialise in treating psychological disorders, is rumoured to report on the true mental condition of an apparently perfectly well balanced member of the Cabinet. Unconfirmed reports..."

Silence in the car. Quinn taking in what he has been told.

Quinn Do I understand you?

Trafalgar Move the pervert to his endgame.

Quinn The stakes are high.

Trafalgar The stakes are what they are. Between prison and social ruin the doctor's got one route out. Lead him to it.

Quinn What does he know about Slabb?

Trafalgar He thinks Slabb digs the road. So far as he knows, the only people who know both his identity and his secrets are Slabb, his wife, obviously, and her brother, one of Slabb's cronies. Then there's the woman. Exactly what they all know you'll have to find out yourself. You have to work round them.

Quinn Or with them.

Trafalgar There's no time for brain surgery. Slabb is the most reliable source of information on Republican activity we have. We need him in place. He has to have the report on the Secretary.

Quinn eyes the woman on the bench's legs. He sees that she has now taken an interest in Trafalgar's driver. He follows her gaze.

Quinn New driver?

Trafalgar Not seen him before?

Quinn What happened to the other guy?

Trafalgar Drivers come and go.

PAUSE

Quinn Slabb, what does he say?

Trafalgar He's not ready to be retired. He'll work with you.

Quinn What does he know?

Trafalgar Nothing. You're a man with no history. No existence.

Quinn Not to you.

Trafalgar I'm not making myself clear. What's it to be? Back inside... this time for life?

Quinn Framed once, framed twice. You make it sound like a choice.

Trafalgar We're all framed, Quinn. One way or another. It's called life. One last thing... The woman. Her mind has gone. Stay away from her. She fouls this up and you know where you'll be spending the rest of your days.

5. White City

Tuesday. Midday. A workman's hut. Slabb's HQ.

A tin hut stands at the end of a dead end street. It is set up outside a row of falling down houses. With its back to the factory wall that blocks off the street it can only be approached from one direction; in sight of the men sitting inside it. A workman's hut, it stands in a street that has no work going on.

Quinn walks down the dusty street. The sun overhead. The sky blue. Birds singing. The man standing outside the hut watching him approach.

>**Slabb** Quinn?
>
>**Quinn** Yes.
>
>**Slabb** You one of us?
>
>**Quinn** It's a name.
>
>**Slabb** There's blood in a name.
>
>**Quinn** Maybe. Way back.
>
>**Slabb** Blood goes back.

They stoop and enter the darkness of the hut. The smell and smoke of food just fried. At the end of the hut Weed manhandling a pan over a gas burner. Weed looks up at Quinn from behind thick lenses that enlarge his eyes.

Slabb indicates one of two wooden planks supported on oil drums. Partially obscured lettering around the waist of the drums seems to read 'Castrol'. Quinn takes his seat.

Quinn Who's this?

Slabb Weed. He's with me. He knows what there is to know.

Weed And who are you Quinn, and what do you know? And what's the reason this boss man whoever picked you to help us out? You the brave zookeeper who has to get in the cage with us animals and feed us cause we can't do it ourselves, is that it?...

Slabb You shut up. I said I'll do the talking...*(to Quinn)* Ignore this fool.

Quinn looks at the brightness outside. A small bird crosses in front of the hut, takes off.

Quinn Nothing from the doctor?

Slabb He's stalling.

Quinn When did you last see Helen Suter?

Slabb Who?

Quinn Helen Suter. Your contact with Doctor Fairfax.

Slabb Looby Loo?

Quinn Did you just say Looby Loo?

Slabb That's what she calls herself. That's what we call her.

Quinn You know she's one of his patients?

Slabb That's how this works.

Quinn You know her real name?

Slabb Lady... whatever... I forget...

Quinn Lady Helen Suter. Her brother's The Marquis of Tintagel.

Weed Some lady.

Slabb Tintagel? Isn't that fairyland?

Quinn Could be this is fairyland.

Slabb Not to me. Brady's no fairy. I need that piece of paper. By Saturday and in the real world... Why's The Doc stalling now, on this one?... Can you tell me that?

Quinn The Secretary? This has to go off right. This has to be his last play.

Slabb I need to get it off him before he makes that play.

Quinn Only he knows where it is...

Slabb We already asked him.

Quinn Only he can produce it...We show him how he can do it, make one hit and be free of all his problems.

Slabb A hit... what's this idea?

Quinn You and the doctor have to meet. He brings the report. You surrender the snaps. His reputation, his career, is safe. The only people who know that he's been stealing the medical reports are all gone.

Slabb That's not an idea I like the sound of.

Quinn Ideas never killed anyone.

Slabb Is this idea idea your idea?

Quinn Trafalgar's.

Slabb Arrange my assassination. Weed gets it too most likely. Cathleen probably. That's all Trafalgar's idea?

Quinn Trafalgar's idea is get Brady off your back. Fast. You stay put where he needs you. The doctor's in a deep hole. The chance to silence you and get away with it is his one window. We open it.

Slabb And he steps right through it. Into me.

Quinn Talk.

Slabb Never killed anyone?

Weed *[to Slabb]* Trafalgar needs you? What does that mean? I thought you...

Slabb What is wrong with you? I told you all about him. Only yesterday. Have you forgotten since then?...*[to Quinn]* Alright.

Quinn This Looby Loo, when did you last see her?

Slabb Not for a couple of days. She gets around.

Quinn She playing straight?

Slabb How d'you mean?

Quinn She's already got the report. Making her own plans?

Slabb She knows what I'd do to her.

Weed Don't count on it, mister. She's too far gone to know what's dangerous and what isn't. Even if she knew she wouldn't care.

Quinn Is he right?

Slabb The Doc's the problem, not her.

Quinn What does she know about you?

Slabb She knows which side we're on. It's no secret. She doesn't know what we do.

Quinn The doctor steals or copies the medical records on a name she's given him. He gives it to her and she gives it straight to you?

Slabb How much do you need?

Quinn The whole picture.

Slabb What she gets she brings straight to me.

Quinn What's in it for her?

Slabb She gets paid.

Quinn Who by?

Slabb Me.

Quinn Who does she think is feeding the stuff to the press?

Slabb Me.

Quinn She thinks it's all your idea?

Slabb She thinks it's all her idea.

Quinn It was her idea to screw the doctor into stealing confidential information on government figures?

Slabb That's what she thinks. I didn't say it was the truth.

Quinn She must know what she thinks. How far gone can she be?

Slabb If you saw her you'd see.

Quinn You give her the names?

Slabb Of course.

Quinn You get them?

Slabb From the people who know them.

Quinn You can't tell me.

Slabb You don't mess with these people.

Quinn How do they know?

Slabb How do they know anything?

Quinn The merchandise?

Slabb I make a call. They collect.

Quinn This doctor, Fairfax. What does he think?

Slabb We're thick.

Quinn Meaning?

Slabb We dig the road. Run a shebeen.

Quinn You might have back-up?

Slabb Some thick paddies have back up? Why would he?... Five days, Quinn. There has to be time to call off Brady.

Quinn Four or five days is enough. We put the doctor in a position where he sees his chance but has to make up his mind fast.

Slabb Where does the party happen?

Quinn You tell me. A place known to Fairfax is best. What's this club of yours, The Crypt is it?

Slabb The Crypt... Could work.

Quinn I need to see it.

Slabb You done this sort of thing before? You know what you're doing?

Quinn Tomorrow?

Slabb Whenever. Need anything, let me know...

PAUSE

...Quinn, you don't know my wife.

Quinn Of course not. She worked for the doctor, cleaned his rooms in Harley Street?

Slabb Trafalgar told you?

Quinn That's how the doctor found your drinking club.

Slabb He didn't find it. She told him about it. What he would find there to his taste. He wanted to go. She took him.

Quinn Can I talk to her?

Slabb You can do more than that.

Quinn Meaning?

Slabb She's an accommodating woman. She'd be pleased to see you.

Quinn I'm not with you.

Slabb We're on a mission to save the world, her world. Her job is to keep the troops happy. Understand?

Quinn Possibly.

Slabb Certainly... Quinn, I need that piece of paper.

Quinn *[standing up]* I'll call you. *[Slabb does not get up]*

Weed I'll come with you to the end of the street.

Stooping, Quinn and Weed step out into the brightness. They walk away from the hut.

Weed You're not going to take up that offer are you?

Quinn What's it to you?

Weed She's my sister. That bastard uses her like she's his slave. Loans her out to anyone who can do him a favour. You wouldn't use her yourself would you?

Quinn When could I meet her?

Weed To talk?... The flat... Tomorrow morning. She'll be there.

Quinn Will Slabb be there?

Weed No.

Quinn And you?

Weed I'll be where Slabb is.

Quinn and Weed stand at the end of the street.

Quinn Tell me what you know about Looby Loo.

Weed She's off her trolley. Really going for it.

Quinn Trying to screw the doctor?

Weed Trying to kill herself. By the slowest most painful means she can think of.

Quinn Tell me more. It's important.

Weed Talk to Cathleen about her. I'm not into that crazy tramp... Look, Quinn, I don't know you from Adam. But let me tell you one thing. Slabb's not stupid. He may not be a genius, but he's not stupid.

Quinn You're not stupid yourself, are you Weed?

Weed Me?... I'm alright.

Quinn I know you are. But listen, could you play the fool?

6. White City

Wednesday, 11am. A bedroom in the Slabb flat.

The walkway door to the flat has been left open. Quinn enters.

The bedroom window, which gives on to the walkway, has drawn curtains that do not meet in the middle. In the darkened room a chink of light hits the bed where Cathleen sits. She has on her 'Yes' tee shirt and a floral pattern skirt. She is bare legged and has kicked off a pair of scuffed white mules. On a bedside table a half bottle of Jameson, two tumblers.

Cathleen Quinn? Is that real?

Quinn Enough.

Cathleen You do have a first name?

Quinn Yes.

Cathleen Well, I love a mystery myself. Come and sit down... I don't bite, you know.

Cathleen throws two soft toys down onto the floor and smooths the duvet beside her. The duvet is patterned with rabbits. Quinn sits beside her on the bed.

Quinn Weed's your brother?

Cathleen Hamish.

Quinn Your husband calls him Weed.

Cathleen Treats him like a pet dog. One that he's not that fond of.

Quinn Hamish is fond of you.

Cathleen Yes... Peter Pan.

Cathleen takes the bottle of whiskey off the bedside table, unscrews the top, pours two shots. They clink glasses.

Quinn Hamish...

Cathleen Call him Weed. Everyone else does.

Quinn He said Looby Loo was trying to kill herself. That she was crazy. Is she?

Cathleen Crazy? Or trying to kill herself?

Quinn Either.

Cathleen I wouldn't say she was crazy. She might be trying to kill herself.

Quinn How well do you know her?

Cathleen We talk now and then. We've one or two things in common.

Quinn Such as?

Cathleen Little girls lost, wouldn't you say?

She pours more whisky for herself without her glass being empty.

Quinn In what way are you lost?

Cathleen Any way you care to think of. Did I want this life? Living in this dump. Playing Michael's whore. Dear God, if Ma could see what I've done in my time she'd kill herself. If Pa could see, he'd kill me. Letting them down, that's what upsets Hamish so.

She looks into Quinn's eyes then runs a finger over the

bruises on her arms...

...You're wondering why... I didn't get these falling over.

Quinn What does Weed say about that?

Cathleen One day. Going to be a hero, rescue me from all this. Take me back to the village where we grew up and me and him will parade through the streets like a homecoming prince and princess. On horseback too, no doubt. Peter Pan and Wendy.

Quinn One day?

Cathleen Better be soon. Or we'll be parading in bathchairs.

Quinn Would you go?

Cathleen Don't think about it. Too painful.

Quinn I'm sorry.

Cathleen Chose it, didn't I? Dug my own grave. Now I've got to lie in it.

Quinn I thought you didn't choose it.

Cathleen Didn't know what I was choosing. I was a little girl...

Drinks, stares at him over the rim of her glass.

...Still am, don't you think?... In some ways, maybe?

Quinn Is Helen the same?

Cathleen Someone who calls herself Looby Loo is a mature well balanced grown up?

Quinn What's she looking for?

Cathleen Herself if you ask me.

Quinn Sounds more like she's running from herself.

Cathleen Can't find herself. Looked everywhere, so she thinks, and found nothing. Now she's standing on the edge seeing if the wind will blow her off... It will do soon... *[pause]* Who are you Quinn? What are we to you?

Quinn A lifeline.

Cathleen What does that mean?

Quinn Does it matter what it means? I'm here to help you and Michael.

Cathleen Would it were one and the same thing.

Quinn This Brady...

Cathleen Donal.

Quinn Someone you know?

Cathleen I did know a boy called Donal. Once. He loved me. Or at least he said he did.

Quinn What happened?

Cathleen Michael. Spoilt for choice, wasn't I? By the way, I was beautiful then, Quinn.

Quinn I can believe it.

Cathleen I've still nice eyes, haven't I Quinn? Don't they sparkle?... Well, don't they?

Quinn I don't know what to say.

Cathleen Say what you think. Only don't make fun.

Quinn They do sparkle, yes.

Cathleen I know they do.

Quinn You chose Michael?

Cathleen I chose wrong. It's something I do.

Quinn Brady's a killer.

Cathleen Maybe he never would have been if I'd said yes. As I was meant to. But you're right. He went bad.

Maybe, in a way, like me and Looby Loo.

Quinn And if all of this doesn't work out, and he does come?

Cathleen What will be will be. I'd heard say he'd gone soft. Lost the will.

Quinn It doesn't seem so. After last weekend.

Cathleen Who knows? Nobody tells the truth any more, Quinn. All that comes out of people's mouths is stories. Sometimes I can't be bothered believing or not believing anybody or anything. Sometimes I think I'll just sit here, do nothing and wait and see what actually happens.

Quinn moves to stand up. Cathleen presses his thigh back onto the mattress. Gestures with her glass.

Quinn Go on then.

Cathleen[*pouring*] You haven't touched me, Quinn. Don't you like what you see?

Quinn I do like what I see.

Cathleen What then?

Quinn This isn't how I'd do it.

Cathleen No. You're a gentleman.

Quinn There's not many who'd agree with that.

Cathleen I've known a lot of men in my time. And you can believe that. I know a gentleman when I'm with one.

Quinn Well, thank you.

Cathleen Touch me, Quinn. You can you know...

Quinn puts his hand inside her tee shirt, caresses her

breasts.

Cathleen Nice boobs aren't they? Not that bad?

Quinn kisses her on the lips. Her lips are soft and wet. He sees her look over his shoulder. He turns to see Weed's face at the window, peering through the gap in the curtains. Cathleen shoos him away with a wave of her hand.

Quinn leaves her sitting on the bed, her soft toys back on the pillow. He lets himself out. Weed meets him at the bottom of the stairs. He has been waiting under one of the cherry trees.

Quinn Do you always spy on your sister?

Weed She's my sister. I have to watch out for her.

Quinn You're right. You do.

Weed Well?

Quinn Well what?

Weed Well what was the matter?... Don't you like her? Isn't she your type or something?

Quinn Of course I do.

Weed Bloody right. She's a beautiful woman.

Quinn Yes.

Weed You haven't upset her have you? You didn't turn her down, did you?

Quinn Why would I want to do that?

Weed She upsets easily. She's my sister. I worry about her.

Quinn I know you do.

7. White City

Wednesday. Midday. Quinn and Weed among the tower blocks.

They are on their way to The Crypt. Weed's leg has 'gone gammy' and every 100 yards he stops, leans against a wall and flexes his ankle. He is wearing heavy work boots and this is a difficult, nearly impossible operation. He makes faces at passers-by who look at him performing his 'looseners'. When they are out of earshot he swears after them and then turns to stare at the next comer who wonders who he is swearing at.

Soon they cut into a small public garden. They stop at a bench half covered by overgrown rhododendron. It seems to be a familiar place to Weed. Behind the bush is a high wire fence and behind that an infants' school. From the school comes the sound of a steel band. The opening bars of 'Three Blind Mice' are played over and over, each time with the mistake on a different note.

Weed *[sitting on the bench]* Bad today. Gotta give it five.

Quinn Sure.

Weed undoes the laces down several eyelets and kicks the boots off.

Weed These boots. Can't break 'em in. They're the real McCoy.

Quinn Where did you get them?

Weed Dead man's shoes.

Quinn How so?

Weed Found them in the street. Must have fallen off a pick up. What a result. Good as new.

Quinn Your size?

Weed Nearly.

Quinn But they hurt.

Weed Can't have everything. Just think, some poor sod can't figure out where he's left his new boots. Must be digging the road in his slippers. Magic... Christ, hope he doesn't see me and recognise them.

Quinn Could be he knows exactly where he left them.

Weed What does that mean?

Quinn Could be he threw them away because they hurt his feet.

Weed *[stares at Quinn]* Don't talk soft.

Quinn Do you put up with everything that's no good for you?

Weed What's this?

Quinn A question.

Weed I know what I'm doing.

Quinn With Slabb?

Weed Yeah with Slabb. That's what you mean isn't it?

Quinn Cathleen too.

Weed Well that's it isn't it? I can't do what I would do, or could do, on account of her.

Quinn You have to look out for her?

Weed Someone has to. I'm her brother.

Quinn That makes it your duty to stay?

Weed Doesn't it? What kind of man are you?

Quinn I don't know. I haven't got a sister.

Weed Well lucky you. You're a free agent. Some of us have got responsibilities. Do the right thing and all.

Quinn You didn't tell her to marry Slabb did you?

Weed Did I fuck? I warned her. Slabb's a bastard, I said, it's well known.

Quinn She ignored you?

Weed Doesn't everyone? She's like everyone.

Quinn Then she can't expect you to stay and look after her can she?

Weed She's a female isn't she? She's weak. I can't punish her for her mistakes.

Quinn That's pretty noble.

Weed I do my bit. Unlike that bastard.

Quinn Why does she stay with him?

Weed You want to ask her that.

Quinn I did.

Weed What did she say?

Quinn She ignored the question.

Weed See what I mean? You and me both. Jesus, women. What are they for, does anyone know?

Quinn You can't do anything till she decides to leave Slabb?

Weed She won't do that.

Quinn Frightened of him?

Weed You'd think so, but no.

Quinn What then?

Weed Frightened of doing wrong. Someone up there might punish her. Doesn't want to go to hell.

Quinn Your sister believes in heaven and hell?

Weed Why wouldn't she? Truth is, she knows she's bought her ticket already. Immoral behaviour. First degree. She's just hoping if she now becomes the dutiful wife she might get a reprieve.

Quinn Isn't that a bit mixed up?

Weed Try telling her. Look, she's a woman, like I say. She's all over the place. One day she hates him. The next day he's only doing it because it's his way of looking after her and me.

Quinn Any truth in that?

Weed What? Do I need looking after?... Kidding or what?

Quinn So where's it going to end?

Weed Am I a Druid?

Quinn Your hands are tied.

Weed You said it.

Quinn What about this Brady?

Weed You know about him?

Quinn Everyone knows about him. I'm talking about him and her.

Weed She told you a lot then. She must like you.

Quinn We get on.

Weed I can't understand why you didn't...

Quinn You didn't want me to, remember?

Weed Yeah, but when it's on a plate, and it's steaming hot?

Quinn What's her idea about Brady?

Weed She didn't tell you?

Quinn She said 'What will be will be.'

Weed Can't say fairer than that.

Quinn Slabb scared of him?

Weed*[smiles]* Big time. He's shitting himself, and you can bet that's not a pretty sight. Can you imagine what Brady might do to Slabb if, let's say, he gets wind of what he puts her through for his own amusement?

Quinn Brady still cares for Cathleen?

Weed What Brady cares for is killing. He doesn't need an excuse. Punishing Slabb is plenty... Slabb's desperate for that report, take it from me. He's got to be sure Brady never crosses the Irish Sea.

Quinn Brady comes, what do you do?

Weed Depends on her.

Quinn You'd be free.

Weed There's a chance... Are you going to get that report for Slabb?

Quinn I have to.

Weed That's it isn't it? You and me both. And every other bugger. No-one's free to do what they want. Do as you're told or screw yourself. Big time. *[pause]* What are you doing here, Quinn?... Really, I mean? Who are you?

Quinn You asked me that before.

Weed I still want to know.

Quinn You know why I'm here.

Weed This Trafalgar, what's he got on you?

Quinn We're on the same side, Weed.

Weed What side is that?

Quinn Trafalgar's I guess.

Weed Me, I don't like guessing. I'm not a gambler.

Quinn Slabb and Looby Loo, they get on?

Weed Far as I know they hardly speak. But what do I know? It's only yesterday I found out there's someone walking around who can put me, all of us, inside at the click of his fingers.

Quinn Trafalgar?

Weed Never even heard of him till yesterday. Cathleen neither. That's how much we know. The sheer tonnage of what I don't know about my own life is scary.

Quinn Listen, Weed, do you know everything about what Slabb does?

Weed Such as?

Quinn Let's say... do you think his commanders know everything he does?

Weed These are some strange questions.

Quinn What do they know about Trafalgar?

Weed How should I know? ...I guess they know everything. They know everything else don't they?

Quinn Like Trafalgar?

Weed Why don't you ask Slabb?

Quinn That's a very good question. The answer is I'd rather get it from you.

Weed But why?

Quinn I trust you. That's why... This Looby Loo. Why does Slabb use her? She's a risk isn't she?

Weed Got to be something between them, but I don't get it.

Quinn Is he fucking her?

Weed No.

Quinn She fucks anyone doesn't she?

Weed Slabb doesn't go with any woman.

Quinn Not even Cathleen?

Weed Not any more.

Quinn Why not?

Weed Have a guess. Go on. A really wild one.

Quinn She's impure or something?

Weed Madness, right? Big time. It's where he's going. In his mind she's turned into a whore who enjoys it.

Quinn When he made her what she is.

Weed Got to blame someone. I'm only surprised it's not my fault. Probably it is, only I haven't been told yet.

Quinn He's not just scared of Brady. He's jealous.

Weed In one.

Quinn Because she has thoughts about him?

Weed He can't accuse her of being a whore with Brady. She hasn't seen him for years. Part of him wants her to fuck him as soon as he gets here.

Quinn To make Brady just one of the others?

Weed It's the way his mind works. But it doesn't of course.

Quinn Well how does it?

Weed Truth is he's jealous of all of them. Of you. If you sleep with her. And I tell you something else...

Quinn She knows it?

Weed In one.

Quinn Which gives her something over Slabb.

Weed Bull's eye.

Quinn Which is why Slabb says she enjoys it?

Weed And which is why she knows she's going to hell.

Quinn Because she enjoys it?

Weed Because she knows she's toying with him. Makes sense doesn't it?

Quinn If you're Irish.

Weed We are Irish... So should you be with a name like Quinn.

Quinn And you?

Weed What about me?

Quinn You slept with Looby Loo?

Weed I don't sleep with women.

Quinn Why not?

Weed They don't want me.

Quinn Not even Looby Loo?

Weed Not even her.

Quinn Like you say... can't have everything. Your foot rested?

Weed Yeah, thanks.

Quinn How far is it?

Weed stands up, points through the gardens beyond the school to where an alleyway runs to garages and workshops at the foot of a tower block.

Weed That's it over there.

8. White City

Wednesday pm. The tin hut.

Outside, a violent rainstorm. A black sky. Inside it is near pitch.

Quinn, Slabb and Weed in conference. Quinn with a large plastic 'Woolworth' bag at his feet. Slabb hands Quinn a rag. He wipes his head and neck.

Water sluices into drains. The rain drills into the tin over their heads. The men speak with raised voices.

Quinn We keep this simple. This depends on Weed, how good he is.

Slabb Simpler the better then. Hey, Quinn, when did I agree to my future depending on this halfwit?

Quinn You've seen The Godfather?

Slabb Have I been to the pictures?

Weed Five times, me.

Slabb I saw The Wizard of Oz too. Twice, I think.

Quinn Did you get it?... The scene in the restaurant. The guy goes to the toilet picks up a gun that's been left there and comes back and shoots the guy he left at the table?

Slabb So?

Quinn We copy it.

Slabb How clever is that? The Doc's seen it too. Ten times probably. How does that work?

Quinn Everyone's seen it.

Slabb And?

Quinn Everyone knows it works. That includes The Doc.

Slabb Works for us is what I'm asking.

Quinn The Doc only comes to this meet if he knows he can walk away from it. It's all working for him.

Slabb The Doc's no fool, Quinn. Yeah, he's got himself in a mess but he's no fool.

Quinn We cover every angle he's going to think of.

Slabb He's going to think of all of them.

Quinn Weed puts the idea of the meet to him. He shows him he can do this and get away with it. Not just that he might be able to kill you, because how's he going to do it? He might take a year to decide. Or he might bottle out and run. He has to decide you have to be with the fairies by Saturday night. Weed tells his part right, the story goes right. But there has to be a reason why Weed's putting himself on the line.

Slabb Because he knows about the blackmail?

Quinn And he'll know, for a fact, that Doctor Fairfax was your killer. Saturday night, when the party's over, there either has to be no-one left who knows the truth or else anyone who knows and is still alive is no threat.

PAUSE.

Weed What's in that bag?

Quinn See for yourself.

Quinn picks up the Woolworth bag from between his feet, hands it to Weed.

Weed Something nasty?

Quinn See for yourself.

Weed reaches into the bag, pulls out two smaller heavy duty plastic bags. He opens one, looks inside. 'Jesus, man.'

Slabb Well, what is it?

Weed A gun.

Weed lifts into view the shiny blue-black body, slatey barrel and checkered redwood grip of a snub nose revolver.

Quinn Colt. In.38 Special. It's not loaded.

Quinn takes the Colt from Weed's hands, releases the cylinder catch and drops out the cylinder to show them the six empty chambers. He pushes the cylinder back in place and hands the Colt back to Weed.

Slabb Where did you get that?

Quinn You know my supplier. *[To Weed]* Get the feel of it. You're going to have to get used to it.

Weed Neat.

Weed turns the gun over up and around in his hands.

Quinn Weed, you don't point that thing at people. Even when it's not loaded. They tend to get the wrong idea... I see you're not used to handling weapons.

Slabb It's not our line.

Quinn I thought it was what you did.

Slabb Materials, transport, beds. That we sort. Not hardware.

Quinn It's not a problem. It's not either of you two that'll be using it. Doctor Fairfax was in Korea. He knows how to shoot.

Slabb Do you know that for a fact?

Quinn Argyll and Sutherland Highlanders. It's in the books... Look, this gun is easy to get the hang of. It's a Cobra...

Weed You just said it was a Colt.

Quinn Cobra is the model. Colt is the make. See the horse, pony, whatever, on the side?

Weed Oh yeah, neat.

Quinn Neat is it. Aluminium frame so it's lightweight. Two inch barrel, it'll go in your pocket. Or the doctor's. Now look in the other bag.

Weed puts down the gun, opens the other bag. Two small cardboard boxes. One red, one black, both unmarked. Quinn holds out his hand and Weed gives him the two boxes. Quinn opens the red box, shows Slabb and Weed the dull gold and pink contents. A remaining half load of brass cartridges with copper jacketed noses.

Box number one, ten live rounds. These cartridges are .38 Specials. The same calibre that killed those four men Saturday.

He opens the second, black box... contents seemingly the same.

...Box number two, ten dummy rounds. .38 Specials the same as in the other box. These don't go bang. No one gets hurt. These are from the same box as the live rounds but these loads have been taken apart and reassembled with the powder and primer removed. The stamps and markings are the same. The primer hasn't been fired. The cartridge heads look identical.

He picks up one live cartridge and one dummy round and holds them in his open palm.

...The dummy round has scratch markings on the side of the brass casing so that you yourself can tell them apart. Other than that there's no difference. The dummy has a filling in the case so as to match the weight and feel of the live rounds.

Quinn picks up the Colt, thumbs the cylinder catch and swings out the cylinder again. He takes the live cartridge and loads it. Then he loads the dummy round in the next chamber. He spins the cylinder and shows it to Slabb and Weed again.

...Can you tell which is which?... You can't.

Quinn tips up the gun and empties both rounds into his palm. Now he returns the live round to the red box and then reloads the dummy round into one of the chambers. He picks up five more of the dummy rounds and slots them into the other chambers. He shows Slabb and Weed the fully stocked cylinder then clicks it shut. With the cylinder closed he turns the Colt in his hand showing them the visible cartridge rims in the cylinder and, from the business end, bullet noses in the chambers.

Quinn To look at this is a loaded gun. Ready to go.

Slabb Is this a cabaret with magic or an attempted execution?

Quinn Weed shows Doctor Fairfax the gun and the box of live rounds. Saturday night it will be left loaded in some place in The Crypt previously agreed with him. Stick with Hollywood and say the toilet. Just how you and he work the details of the exchange will have to be negotiated. Fairfax has to protect himself from you simply punching him in the face and lifting the report... At the due time he arrives with the report on the Secretary. You frisk him. He's clean. You go in. You hand over the photos he wants. Fairfax hands over the report. You start looking the document over. Fairfax says he has to take a leak. He goes to where the gun is hidden. Almost certainly he takes one last look to check that it's loaded. Probably he opens the cylinder but whichever way he checks it, he sees that it is.

Slabb He walks back in and blasts me into the next world? You are a magician. One of the very best.

Quinn He walks back in and shoots you dead with the dummy rounds that Weed has switched for the live ones. You've got the report on the Secretary. You let your people know. Brady stays in Ireland...

PAUSE

Slabb The Doc buys this?

Quinn takes one of the live rounds from the red box, rests it in his palm.

Quinn These slugs are the same calibre as the ones Brady used last weekend in Ireland.

Slabb How?

Quinn Trafalgar... Cartridge cases left at the scene.

.38 Special. The bullets that The Doc will use to finish you are going to be from the same gun that killed the guards in Ireland.

Slabb How will he know that's true?

Quinn He won't know. He'll believe it's true. Weed will make him believe. He'll want it to be true. Because if it is true it's too good to pass up... Weed sells this right, The Doc buys it.

PAUSE

Slabb Where are you in this?

Quinn I have to be there.

Slabb Make sure nothing goes wrong, is that it?

Quinn Must be.

Slabb Where?

Quinn There's nowhere inside. The only place is on the roof. By the skylight over the washroom. If it's left open I can hear what's happening. When The Doc has picked up the gun and gone back to you I'll let myself in and drop onto the work surface. Stay at the back until he tries it.

Slabb Trafalgar?

Quinn Watching.

Slabb Watching us?

Quinn Watching everything. He's set this up. He's watching to see we all do what he says.

Slabb There's a question here. Something not right.

Quinn That question.

Slabb The Doc.

Quinn What Trafalgar says?

45

Slabb Exactly.

Quinn He walks. With the photos.

Slabb Am I getting this? The Doc tries to murder me and I watch him walk out the door?

Quinn This is about that piece of paper. You'll have it. Laugh in his face. Call him names. But you let him walk.

Slabb There's a reason?

Quinn The reason is it's what he wants.

Slabb Trafalgar? But why?

Quinn I don't get to question why. Nor do you.

Slabb Take him later?

Quinn Later.

Slabb But take him?

Quinn Theft of confidential information.

Slabb Why not take him straightaway, at the club?

Quinn Trafalgar's watching. But he isn't there.

Slabb He's not there but you are... Why?

Quinn It's how he wants it.

Slabb Where is Trafalgar then?

Quinn Nowhere. Where he always is.

Slabb What does that mean?

Quinn What it says. Where is he?... Who is he?... Do you know?... Nor does anyone else.

Slabb But you?

Quinn I know what you know. And you know he's watching.

PAUSE

Slabb The Doc gets his day in court. Maybe he'll take me along. For the ride, like?

Quinn What do you know? All Doctor Fairfax knows for sure is that he's been giving the merchandise to Looby Loo. What she did with it he can't be sure.

Slabb He knows The Crypt.

Quinn You run an illegal drinking club that he doesn't want anyone to know he hangs out in. So what?

Slabb The club. That's a stretch on its own.

Quinn Trafalgar.

Slabb He'd sort it?

Quinn You're no use to him inside.

Slabb The pictures. They're taken in the club.

Quinn If he was ready for them to be made public then none of this would be happening. That's what this is about.

Slabb By then he's got nothing to lose.

Quinn Somebody took some embarrassing photos. That's not a crime.

Slabb Blackmail is.

Quinn It wasn't you blackmailing him.

Slabb ...I get it... Let Looby Loo take the hit?... Is this really going to work?

Quinn It worked in the film.

Weed is fondling one of the live rounds, holding the brass casing between his first two fingers and running the top of his thumb over the rounded copper tip of the bullet.

Weed Oh, yeah, it worked alright. In the film the guy came back from the toilet and shot the guy dead.

Quinn You know what I mean.

Slabb One small question, Quinn. Another one. How did you explain Weed going up to the doctor, out of the blue and with this gun, and just handing it over to him and telling him he can kill me if he feels like it? Did I miss that part?

Quinn Weed tells the doctor that he and Cathleen have been plotting to kill you for years. That a certain someone has left a gun with him for safekeeping. That this is the opportunity for everyone to get rid of you.

Slabb stares at Quinn. Outside, the rain does not let up.

9. Harley Street

Wednesday, late afternoon .

The doctor is in his rooms. He is writing up his notes on the last of the day's consultations. His secretary comes in leaving the door open behind her.

Secretary A lady to see you. I told her you are finished for the day but she insists. She says you know her.

Fairfax Well, what's her name?

Secretary She won't give it...

A tall and glamorous looking woman of indeterminate age walks in brushing past the secretary. She is wearing a wide brimmed hat and dark glasses so that her features are hidden. She has on a high end tailored skirt suit that is cut very tight and is too short to be respectable. Her legs are sheathed in sheer nylon seamed stockings and she stands in black patent courts that have an erotically high silver stiletto heel. The woman tells the secretary 'That'll be all thank you', closes the door on her.

Fairfax *[getting to his feet]* I don't believe I've had the pleasure...

Woman There's always a first time, Doctor.

The woman takes off her hat, throws it across the room. She unclips her tightly tucked hair, shakes her head to let free a mass of curls that fall to her shoulders. She takes off her dark glasses.

Fairfax *[laughing]* Where's Looby Loo today?

Helen *[stony faced, with a sneer]* Looking right at you.

Fairfax And she's sober?

Helen Why not?

Fairfax Helen...

Helen Lady Suter to you.

Fairfax Well... have a seat anyway.

Helen looks around the room, chooses the chaise longue by the window. She drapes herself over it, dangling her legs, letting her skirt ride well up her thighs. She watches him eye her legs.

Helen Confused?

Fairfax Certainly... Drink?

Helen I'm here on business.

Fairfax Too bad.

Fairfax goes to wall mounted cabinet. From a decanter he pours himself a very large whisky into a cut glass tumbler.

Fairfax Are you sure you won't?

Helen I get the feeling you prefer me out of my mind. Does it make you feel safer?

Fairfax You're a strange woman, Helen. I don't think I'll ever understand you. Do you know that in spite of all you've put me through, and you know you've as good as wrecked my life, there's still something about you.

Helen My body?

Fairfax The world is full of bodies.

Helen That's the whole problem.

Fairfax Somehow you seem to embody life itself. Somehow you give a man hope.

Helen Enough of flattery... Business.

Fairfax Where did it all go wrong?

Helen Has it?

Fairfax Well, hasn't it?

Helen Perhaps I should ask you the same question.

Fairfax If you did the answer would be easy. What went wrong for me? Meeting you. Until then everything was fine in my world.

Helen Your world was fine? As in fine wine and fine art, is that what you mean? Fine women, were they, that you used to trawl the doorways and alleys of King's Cross for? The same hags you now find in the drinking clubs of White City?

Fairfax A man doesn't choose his own weaknesses.

Helen No. He manages them. You can't. And that's why you're not fine.

Fairfax As fine as you I'd say. But tell me... what do you know about King's Cross and, more to the point, who told you about it?

Helen I don't pretend to be fine. That's the difference.

Fairfax (*angered by the slur and seemingly forgetting his unanswered quest*ion) What's the purpose of this visit? Delivering insults?

Helen Have you lost track? Of what's happening to you? In real life, I mean. I'm here to remind you that we want what you've got. And soon.

Fairfax You'll get it when I'm ready. I want something myself. Before I simply hand it over on demand.

Helen You want something?

Fairfax Information. For instance, who's your contact in the press?

Helen I don't have one.

Fairfax The names, Helen. How come you know who's been treated at the clinics I work in?

Helen Slabb.

Fairfax That sort of information?... Only the press could dig that out. *[pause]* He knows someone?... Or you do.

Helen Does this matter?

Fairfax You want me to cooperate? I need to know who knows what.

Helen Do you think he tells me?

Fairfax You might as well have that drink. We're wasting time.

PAUSE

Helen Alright. It could be some Irish rag. Something in Kilburn is it? I heard that name the other day. I'm not sure. He knows some people. People who know other people.

Fairfax Who gets paid? You or Slabb?

Helen Slabb.

Fairfax It's you I give the information to.

Helen I give it to Slabb. He delivers to whoever it

is. He gets paid by whoever. He doesn't tell me. I don't ask. What do I care?

Fairfax I care.

Helen What does it matter how any of this happens? What counts is that it is happening and that you don't seem to be keeping up. Slabb's got the snaps of you roughing it in The Crypt with your old hags. You've got the report on the Secretary. If you don't want it to be your name your face, and your personal details in the Sunday papers you know what to do... It's all so simple.

Fairfax Slabb will get his report.

Helen So why stall?

Fairfax I'm fed up with being pushed around by that moron. You heard what I said on Monday. When he offers me the photos, directly, and I mean all of them, then he'll see the report. Tell him that.

Helen Now you talk... The Secretary. Did I give you his name?... No I didn't. I didn't even know who the Secretary of State for Northern Ireland was. I didn't care. I don't care. Slabb says he didn't give you his name.

Fairfax That is true. Yes.

Helen You found and stole the file on the Secretary when you didn't have to?

Fairfax But I did have to. I needed something to bargain with. I looked and I got it. Maybe that was my piece of luck... By the way, you can tell Slabb from me that it's worth waiting for. The Secretary won't survive it.

Helen Enough of this pantomime. I'll take that drink.

Fairfax Of course.

Fairfax pours her a measure of whisky from the decanter.

Helen A drink, Doc. Not a rinse.

Fairfax fills the glass, takes the decanter and sits next to her on the chaise longue. She knocks back half the glass in one, coughs violently. She downs the rest of the glass, holds it out for a refill. Fairfax tops up.

Helen I'm going. You've wasted enough of my time.

Fairfax puts his hand on her knee, slides it up her thigh pushing her skirt up higher.

Fairfax We're in a mess. Both of us. But we can work this out... You know, you look stunning Helen. You should dress like this more often.

Helen You and me? Forget it, Doc. I'm definitely not your type. Don't insult me with that again. Come back when I'm older than my mother. I'll take my teeth out to suck you off.

Fairfax The drink's working wonders. Even in those clothes you're quite a bitch.

Helen Like I said I'm here on business, not pleasure. Not that doing it with you would be any sort of pleasure...

10. INTERMISSION

Wednesday, late afternoon. Harley St.

Helen Suter stands at the top of the steps to Fairfax's building. The street door clicks shut behind her. She puts on her hat at a rakish tilt. It floats on her mass of curls. The high fashion suit, nylons and spiked heels combine with her wild hair to create a stunning apparition. She looks ready for anything. Within seconds any number of passing cars and trucks toot their horns at her.

Quinn is waiting in the street in a rented Ford. He recognises her as the woman who went into the building twenty minutes before. He guesses that this must be Helen Suter, even though Trafalgar gave him no photo of her. He starts the motor.

Helen Suter hails a cab and climbs in. Fifty yards behind the cab Quinn pulls out from the kerb. As he does a parked BMW saloon pulls out between him and the cab.

The cab leaves Harley at the south end, takes Cavendish Square and crosses Oxford into Bond. The BMW and the Ford sit with it. The cab turns west out of Bond, crawls through Berkeley Square, leaves by Curzon and out into Park Lane. From Hyde Park Corner it heads through Belgrave Square and pulls up at the corner of Eaton Place and Lyall Street. The BMW passes the cab and pulls in forty yards further on. Quinn stops the Ford short of the cab.

Helen Suter pays off the cab and walks into the entrance to a mews. Quinn drives into the mews in time to see her mass of curls disappear into the back door of the corner house. Quinn parks up in Lyall Street, from where he can see into the mews as well as see the main door of the house.

An hour and a half later Helen Suter reappears in the mews. Now though she has on her usual street uniform of leather and boots. She is obviously drunk, staggering in her high heels over the cobbles of the mews. In Eaton Square she falls into the back of a cab. The cab turns west towards Kings Road. Quinn hangs back. The BMW tucks in behind the cab as it queues to get into Sloane Square.

Twenty minutes of traffic later, in Sands End, the cab pulls up outside a dilapidated terraced house off the Wandsworth Bridge Road. She falls out of the cab, staggers to the door and lets herself in. It is still daylight but a light comes on upstairs and the curtains are drawn. Quinn follows the BMW as it pulls away.

ACT 2

11. White City

Thursday am. The bench by the infants' school.

Quinn and Weed listening to endless choruses of 'Old MacDonald'. Weed's workboots surrounded by a pile of half-smoked cigarettes. At a high window in the infants' school kids can be seen finger painting.

Quinn You okay?

Weed Course.

Quinn Seeing The Doc later?

Weed Jesus.

Quinn Something bothering you?

Weed This is going to happen?

Quinn That depends on you. Why?

Weed Nothing... Slabb.

Quinn What about him?

Weed Nothing... Something's up with him.

Quinn What?

Weed He's in a sulk.

Quinn Over what?

Weed Won't say.

Quinn He won't or you won't?

Weed He won't.

Quinn Have you said something to him?

Weed Me? No... Nothing more than I always say.

Quinn Which is what?

Weed Nothing... Just me and Cathleen have had enough of him and this fucking country.

Quinn And?

Weed That's what I mean. Normally he just laughs in our faces and says 'Go on, then. See how far you get. You won't even make Euston Station,' or some such. This time he's decided he's taking it personal. Stopped speaking to us. Gone all silent.

Quinn What's that about?

Weed Can't say. Could be Brady I suppose.

Quinn That he's coming? That's nothing to do with you.

Weed Not that he's coming.

Quinn What then?

Weed He's got this thing in his head we want him to come. Especially Cathleen. He's acting hurt. We don't respect him. Look at all he's done for us. Where would we be if it wasn't for him? We take him for granted. You know the stuff.

Quinn Big baby then.

Weed Big baby, big time.

Quinn Comical.

Weed It would be if he didn't mean it. I don't know what he might do.

Quinn What might he do?

Weed He gets emotional he goes OTT, big time, know what I mean? Loses it... one way or another.

Quinn What are you saying?

Weed Could be he'll pull the plug on this whole

thing.

Quinn Throw away the chance to stop Brady from coming, which is what he wants?

Weed I'm not saying he will. I'm saying he could.

Quinn Makes no sense. Hurt himself to spite you and Cathleen.

Weed Can't tell with him. He's got it in him to do it is all I'm saying. Is it genuine or is it an act? Who can tell?

Quinn If you can't, I can't.

Weed Is he hurt or is he calculating?

Quinn Calculating what?

Weed Maybe, you know, Brady comes, the three of us dumped in a bog somewhere. He's got us where he wants us, having to start again, having to rely on him to survive. Is that his game? Well, is it? I don't know.

Quinn He might just not show or something, go AWOL?

Weed Done it before. Disappeared for five days. We thought he'd been murdered.

Quinn What happened?

Weed Gone walkabout. After a bust up with Cathleen.

Quinn Where did he go?

Weed This'll kill you. The Norfolk Broads.

Quinn Come on.

Weed Yeah, I know. Tell me about it.

Quinn Is he an artist or something?

Weed He's something. Big time.

Quinn Well, whatever he is you'd better make up. The pair of you. Before Saturday.

Weed We've got our pride too you know. It's just another way of pushing us around.

Quinn What is this, kindergarten? Do you want Brady to come? *[Weed doesn't answer.]* Do you want to be dumped in that bog with Slabb and Cathleen? You'll never get away. Your best chance is here, Weed. One day you'll break free. Maybe soon. Quite soon.

Weed Yeah, that's right. It could happen.

Quinn You need this meet as much as Slabb does. This report... It's your ticket as much as his.

Weed You're right.

Quinn Has Cathleen said something to you?

Weed Such as?

Quinn I don't know. Something's different about you.

Weed I'm nervous I guess. Jesus.

Quinn You haven't got to do anything. Just talk to Fairfax, tell him what I told you to tell him. What's there to be nervous about?

Weed Yeah. You're right. Nothing. This meet... I mean... It couldn't go wrong or anything could it? I mean... you know.

Quinn No, I don't know.

Weed Something, maybe, could happen wrong. Things do, don't they? I don't know, the gun or something...

Quinn Sometimes.

Weed Yeah. You're right. Sometimes. Things can go wrong is all I'm saying... No. You're right. This meet has to happen. You're right, Jesus. This is everybody's big chance. Sod Slabb.

Quinn Make it happen Weed.

Weed It's up to The Doc isn't it?

Quinn And Slabb.

Weed Yeah. And Slabb. He better play. Or else.

Quinn And Cathleen.

Weed Cathleen. Her too. You're right.

Quinn And you.

Weed Yeah. And me. You're right.

12. Regent's Park

Thursday. Noon. Interior of a Rolls Royce Silver Shadow. Fairfax at the wheel. Weed on the back seat, the Woolworth bag beside him.

A sunny day. The car parked close by the American Ambassador's Residence. Sunk down in the soft leather of the back seat Weed can look out and see tennis courts where middle aged women with tanned legs are playing in extra short white skirts. Apart from the ticking of the car clock, quiet in the car. The sounds of outside deadened by the sealed windows. Fairfax turns in the seat to look back at Weed.

Fairfax You called this meeting, if that's what this is. What is it you want to say?

Weed Got a cigarette?

Fairfax passes over a pack of Camel filters. Weed takes one, starts to take a second.

...Okay to keep the pack?

Fairfax Can't you get anything for yourself?

Weed It's nothing to you, Doc. What, a pack of cigs is gonna break you?

Fairfax It's nothing to you either, truth be told.

Weed Kidding or what?... Got a light?

Fairfax lights Weed's cigarette from the dash.

Fairfax What's this about?

Weed You know of course.

Fairfax I didn't ask to see you.

Weed Nice wheels. What's it worth, twenty, thirty?

Fairfax What's the difference?

Weed A lifetime.

Fairfax Has Slabb got his eyes on this?

Weed You know what Slabb wants.

Fairfax You don't deny that it's Slabb who has been putting Helen Suter up to all this?

Weed Who's denying it?

Fairfax She did. Looby Loo as she calls herself. Until yesterday. Why?

Weed Ask her.

Fairfax I did. She said Slabb told her to. Why?

Weed Ask him.

Fairfax He's not here is he?

Weed We've missed you, Doc.

Fairfax You expect me to come to The Crypt while you're blackmailing me?

Weed Business, Doc, not personal.

Fairfax Did Slabb tell you to say that?

Weed It's the truth.

Fairfax Say what you've got to say.

Weed Slabb wants to meet. Right away.

Fairfax What does he want?

Weed The file on the Secretary. You get your party snaps. You two kiss goodbye. The whole thing is finished.

Fairfax He got my message?

Weed Message?

Fairfax I told Looby Loo to tell him I wanted to trade.

Weed Looby Loo knows about this?... I don't get this.

Fairfax What is it you're not getting?

Weed I don't know... Something... Anyway, he wants to trade.

Fairfax So he says.

Weed So he says.

Fairfax Can I believe him?

Weed If you want to. Do you want to?

Fairfax You hardly seem to believe it yourself.

Weed I'm just the messenger.

Fairfax He hasn't spoken to Looby Loo?

Weed We haven't seen her for days.

Fairfax You haven't or he hasn't?

Weed Neither of us... But you have?

Fairfax Does Slabb tell you everything?

Weed He tells me what he wants to tell me. How can I tell if it's everything?... This is what I'm trying to get at.

Fairfax You're losing me.

Weed Look, Doc, Slabb sent me here to give you a message. But I've got a message of my own.

Fairfax I'm listening.

Weed Do you think Slabb and me are the best of friends?

Fairfax I couldn't say.

Weed You know the way he treats my sister, the way he treats me.

Fairfax You're both still there, aren't you?... Anyway, what can you do about it?

Weed I'm coming to that.

Fairfax How long are you going to take?

Weed Help me out, Doc. I'm trying to be straight with you. This whole thing has been nothing to do with me. It's something Looby Loo and Slabb got up themselves. At first me and Cathleen didn't even know about it. Seems like it was Looby Loo dreamt the whole thing up, got Slabb to agree.

Fairfax Stealing medical files on public figures. She came up with that?

Weed She's out of it alright, but she's not stupid. She knows you're not loaded. Not big time. What you could steal was worth far more than any cash you could raise... See what I mean? It all makes sense. This is what I'm saying. Business, not personal.

Fairfax Helen told me it's Slabb that gets hold of the names she gives to me. What do you know about that?

Weed Slabb gets the names.

Fairfax He knows someone at some Irish paper. I think she said in Kilburn.

Weed Kilburn's a name.

Fairfax I thought it was a place. The Irish district.

Weed A person.

Fairfax Alright. So this Kilburn, if he actually exists, has a way of finding people who have got something they would rather keep hidden?

Weed Correct.

Fairfax Kilburn is very well connected then.

Weed Must be. By the way, who said he's a he?

Fairfax And now he, or she, has found out about the Secretary of State.

Weed That's not public yet, is it? Not his identity.

PAUSE

Fairfax ...Slabb's big payday?

Weed This one's not for cash.

Fairfax Charity?

Weed You know our politics?

Fairfax Politics?

Weed We're Republicans. Had you figured that out?

Fairfax That's no secret. "Easter 1916!" If I've heard that once I've heard it a hundred times. And as for those songs...

Weed He can't sing, I grant you that.

Fairfax What's politics got to do with it?

Weed Slabb wants to be in with the right people.

Fairfax The IRA?

Weed Wants on the payroll. Been trying for years.

Fairfax And?

Weed Would you want him on your side?

Fairfax They won't have him *[snorts]* ...but then this... document... report... on the Secretary, would be like gold dust to them.

Weed You see it now?

Fairfax They'd be holding the ace.

Weed Big time they would.

Fairfax If they get it.

Weed They know about it they'll get it.

Fairfax And they do know about it?

Weed Ears everywhere, Doc. The walls talk to them.

Fairfax And if Slabb delivers?

Weed His membership card. Set up for life. *[pause]* At least, that's the way he sees it.

Fairfax But you... don't?

Weed Not exactly.

Fairfax A moment ago you said you had your own message for me.

Weed Before I tell you that I want to tell you something about my sister.

Fairfax Cathleen?

Weed She had a lover.

Fairfax I don't mean to be rude, but...

Weed A real lover. Before. Years ago.

Fairfax Before Slabb?

Weed Slabb stole her from this person. She's never forgotten him. He's never forgotten her.

Fairfax Who is this person?

Weed Does the name Donal Brady mean anything to you?

Fairfax The IRA gunman who escaped at the weekend. Four men were killed.

Weed He's the person. Donal and Cathleen. Old flames. It's well documented.

Fairfax And now he's out. Is Slabb worried?

Weed Not as worried as he should be.

Fairfax What does that mean?

Weed They've been writing. Cathleen and Donal. Love letters, you know. Taken up again after all this time... Bout a year ago, more maybe, Slabb lost it and beat up on Cathleen. Bad. Over nothing. She'd had enough, decided to write Brady a letter. Took a chance and put it in the post.

Fairfax The prison?

Weed Portlaoise. The only place for that screwball. They let it go through. They read it of course. He wrote back to her. They let that go too. After they'd read it. This has been going on for a year. Funny thing is Brady can't write. Never learned. Must have got a cell mate to write his love letters for him. I've seen them. Look like an ape wrote them left handed. During a night out on the town. The screws must be pissing themselves.

Fairfax You've seen these letters?

Weed Not all. Some of them are more private than others she says. Not for my eyes. Anyway the last letter says I'm sending you a present soon. You can do what you want with it. We'll see each other soon. Or in heaven anyway. She showed me that one, said what does it mean.

Fairfax That he's coming to get her.

Weed One day anyway.

Fairfax And Slabb?

Weed Get him too. Permanent. He has to pay.

Fairfax Slabb doesn't know about these letters?

Weed Of course not.

Fairfax And did Brady send her a present?

Weed We're all in deep, Doc. Slabb, Cathleen, and

me. And you, Doc. Especially you. How are you going to get out of the hole you're in? Whichever way you turn you're gonna catch it. You know that. Us too. Slabb, for handling stolen documents, for blackmail. Me and Cathleen for being accomplices, even though we're not really. She couldn't do the time. Me neither.

Fairfax What are you saying?

Weed Kill two birds with one stone. Cathleen and me have wanted Slabb out of the way for years. He's had it coming for years. It's only what he deserves. It's just that there's never been a way to do it before. At the same time you cut your way out of the mess you're in. The mess that Slabb put you in. Is he going to chase you for the rest of your life?

Fairfax What was the present Brady sent Cathleen?

Weed passes the Woolworth bag between the seats.

Weed See for yourself.

Fairfax It's a revolver.

Weed Not just any revolver, Doc. This is a very hot piece. This is the gun that killed those four men in Ireland.

Fairfax *[peers over his half moons]* What's your idea?

13. Continuation.

The Rolls Royce. Doctor Fairfax looking out of the window.

Fairfax takes a cloth from the glove compartment, carefully wipes the lenses of his glasses, puts them back on.

Fairfax Might I have one of my own cigarettes?

Weed holds out the pack. Fairfax takes one.

Weed Take two. Go on. One for later.

Fairfax Don't be absurd. *[lights up from the dash]* Suppose I agree...

Weed Saturday night is the last time this can happen.

Fairfax Why Saturday?

Weed They know about it... They're coming to get it.

Fairfax Muscle in on Slabb and Looby Loo's operation?

Weed Sunday they're here... To discuss matters. All polite, like. I can get you an invite.

Fairfax Brady?

Weed Not that maniac. Too much heat. He's holed up... People on this side of the water. Reasonable types. They say good day to you before cutting your balls off... Brady has to wait.

Fairfax How do these... reasonable types... know

it's Slabb they want to see?

Weed Kilburn.

Fairfax Which paper is this, do you know?

Weed No.

Fairfax He doesn't tell you everything then, Slabb I mean?

Weed We've been over this.

Fairfax Kilburn. A false name.

Weed Whatever his name is he wasn't going to say boo to them. No one does. He let us know they'd been to see him. Very sorry and all that but what could we expect?

Fairfax What has he told them?

Weed What he knows, which doesn't include your name. *[pause]* That changes Sunday. Slabb will be showing them your snaps and telling them who you are. Unless, of course, they've already got what they want.

Fairfax This Kilburn. He knows which clinics I work in.

Weed Looby Loo. She got the names of the clinics off your secretary. Like falling off a log, she said. Told the woman she'd told her all her friends about you. There was a chance of plenty more business for you. She gave the names of the clinics to Slabb... "Go digging" Slabb said to Kilburn. The rest we know. Who would have guessed how many sick people there are among the great and the good. Almost like it's a qualification.

Fairfax Being sick?

Weed Or mental. Preferably both. Makes you wonder who's fooling who.

Fairfax Can you be sure Slabb didn't give Kilburn my name?

Weed Didn't offer it. That way he was protecting

his own position. Looby Loo's too. Kilburn was getting the merchandise, he didn't need it... he didn't want it. Otherwise he'd be an accomplice... Slabb does know your name. They won't have to twist his arm much. He's a bully, but he's not brave.

Fairfax The clinics.

Weed How many different doctors work in all the clinics you work in?

Fairfax ...True, I suppose.

Weed So what's it to be?

Fairfax Time.

Weed There isn't any. Let the chance go, it may never come back.

Fairfax The chance to do life... for murder?

Weed Five years max. If it happened... Provocation.

Fairfax You make a funny looking judge. *[pauses]* On second thoughts.. you don't... You say this is the gun that killed those guards? How did Brady get it here?

Weed Every now and then a visitor drops by the Crypt. Unannounced like. Special visitor. Checks everyone's behaving nice. No one's mouthing off about anything they might have been told or heard somehow. Any Irish place gets a visit now and then.

Fairfax To scare people.

Weed To remind them, let's say.

Fairfax You had a visit?

Weed Monday. The gun proves the story, Doc. The bullets will match. They can test that, right?

Fairfax They can tell if two bullets or two cartridge cases have been fired from the same gun. It's not guaranteed though. For them to say definitely it was this particular gun and to match it back to what happened in

Ireland I'd have to leave it in there. It would have my prints on it. I can hardly come back from the toilet wearing gloves.

Weed Your prints on record?

Fairfax Of course not.

Weed Mine are and they're all over this piece. It can't be in there, Doc. This baby's in there, I'm suspect number one not Brady.

Fairfax We could wipe it. Brady's prints would be gone, true, as would yours, but the gun itself together with the bullets and cartridges would make the match. The story would be better.

Weed And if you don't wipe it right?... And are you going to wipe the cartridges too?... Anyway, Brady bothers to wipe the gun and then leaves it there? Doesn't add up. It spoils the story. The gun leaves with us.

Fairfax You and I in the Crypt, Weed. Slabb dead. I'm holding this. And it's loaded.

Weed Kill me too, yeah?... At least it shows you're considering it... Won't work.

Fairfax Cathleen?

Weed Something happens to me you know where she'll go. And you know what she knows. Everything.

Fairfax Where will she be ?

Weed Somewhere you don't know and you can't find. That's our protection from you. This gun can't be in there.

Fairfax Well, what about you and Cathleen?

Weed What about us?

Fairfax How do I know I can trust you? When he's gone I mean.

Weed This is our idea.

Fairfax You say that now...

Weed Of course we say it. This is a new life for us.

Fairfax And when you're free, and in your new life?

Weed Will we come after you?

Fairfax How do I know you won't?

Weed Because by then we're both as guilty as you. Big time. Which is why this works. It cuts both ways. This is a story that's been written with you in mind, Doc. There won't be another.

Fairfax What it is, is a story that hangs on them matching the bullets, which they may not be able to do. More than that. Brady's in hiding, as you just said. They know that. So how did he get here?

Weed They don't know where he is do they? That's the point. It's the gun that's going to show them he's already in England. They won't know how he got here but it will be obvious he is. What this story hangs on is you and us trusting each other. Any one makes a wrong move the other party squeals. The match is made by the facts. The other facts. Brady breaks out, leaves four of these cherries inside four men. A few days later more of these likely from the same box are found inside the man who stole Cathleen from Brady all those years ago and bust up that teenage love story. It's personal and it's all on record. They've been reading his love letters even as he's writing them. In both cases the bullets are fired from a similar gun. Even if there's no exact match chances are they're fired from the same gun. What seems obvious is obvious. There's a homicidal maniac about. And he's bent on revenge. Nobody's asking any more questions...

EXTENDED PAUSE while Fairfax considers...

...Doc, a jury would convict on that. Any jury...

What's bothering you?... Nothing in the world ties you to what happens Saturday. If it happens.

PAUSE

Fairfax Sending this gun to Cathleen. Seems a strange thing to do.

Weed Jesus, Doc. You're still not seeing it. You're just like everyone else. I'm taking the time and you're not listening to me. Brady's jammed up in Ireland. For weeks. Months maybe. A year even. Every port. Every fishing boat, every dinghy. They're watching the waves. He can't even swim across, less he swims underwater.

Fairfax What's that got to do with Cathleen?

Weed What have I been telling you? This gun has special properties. Whoever uses it has nothing to worry about.

Fairfax Brady sent this gun to Cathleen so that she could use it on Slabb?

Weed She couldn't do it. Brady knows that.

Fairfax What then?

Weed Isn't it obvious?

Fairfax He means you to do it?

Weed Me, Cathleen and Brady. We go back. He taught me to skim stones on the lough. Now he's giving me the way to put things right. For her. For me. For good.

Fairfax You and Brady?... An odd couple.

Weed Very odd... I was weak. Still am, in case you hadn't noticed. They picked on me. You can guess... Bad... Easy pickings, you could say. Couldn't see which way the next kick or punch was coming from. Licked me till I couldn't stand up. Brady decided he felt sorry for me. Decided he was gonna look out for me. Warned 'em off. Warned off by the likes of Brady you don't come back. Never... So that's how he and Cathleen... you know.

Fairfax He saw a way into Cathleen's heart.

Weed And the rest of her... So what, if that's what he wanted?

Fairfax Whichever one of you does it... he takes the blame. He must still love her.

Weed I'm not sure if he loves anyone. It could be beyond him.

Fairfax He's her saviour.

Weed He's your saviour too. This gun works the same for you as it would for me or Cathleen. That's why this is so beautiful.

Fairfax Cathleen and Brady. Some story. Can you prove it? Any of it?

Weed I'm giving you known facts, Doc. Prove a known fact is true? Can you prove that heaven and hell exist and that a man with a big white beard sits above the clouds like he does? No, you can't. Everyone else thinks it's true, you have to assume it is and work on that basis.

PAUSE

Fairfax Why then don't you do it yourself?... Brady thinks you can.

Weed I'm not the man I was.

Fairfax Really?

Weed It's been years. I'm blind and I've got the shakes. I couldn't hit the sky. If I could, I would. I'd love the job.

Fairfax It will be point blank.

Weed Do you think I could do it?

PAUSE

Fairfax I've never killed a man.

Weed You've never had to before... You'll be fine.

Fairfax Killing a man in cold blood. An execution.

Weed It's an execution alright. Long overdue. Who said anything about cold blood? I'm fuming, me... Aren't you?

Fairfax I suppose.

PAUSE

Weed What else are you worried about, other than having to do it?

Fairfax Who else knows Slabb's been blackmailing me? Besides Looby Loo.

Weed No-one else.

Fairfax Cathleen?

Weed Well, yes. No-one else.

Fairfax How can I be sure?

Weed I've told no-one.

Fairfax Who's Slabb told? Can you be sure?

Weed Nothing in life is certain. A doctor should know that. We have to act on the odds.

Fairfax The greater the risk the more certain you need to be. You should know that.

Weed The greater the risk the more there is to gain.

Fairfax Or lose.

Weed Not in your case, Doc. That's why this is made for you. You're going down anyway. Sooner or later.

Fairfax I need to know that no-one else knows.

Weed There's no way to prove that.

Fairfax Is Slabb cutting Looby Loo out of this?

Weed What about her? She's a loose end. It's up to you of course. Insist on her being there maybe?

Fairfax Kill her as well?

Weed I don't know. I don't care. It's hard to call. You kill her and it looks less like a revenge killing, know what I mean?

Fairfax Possibly.

Weed She's a tramp, right?

Fairfax Tell Slabb she has to be there.

Weed You agree then?

Fairfax I'm still thinking.

Weed Think up, Doc...

Weed watches Fairfax tidily stub out his cigarette in the ash tray, carefully deliberately close it back into the dash.

...Is it on?

Fairfax Time.

Weed How much?

Fairfax Tomorrow?

Weed Tonight would be better.

Fairfax You're trying to rush me.

Weed It's the facts. You know better than me. You have to operate, you have to operate.

Fairfax I need time.

Weed All afternoon. You have to choose between yes and no.

Fairfax Some choice.

Weed Seven o'clock?

Fairfax Here?

Weed Money for a cab?

14. White City

Thursday. Mid afternoon. The tin hut. Slabb and Weed.

Slabb cooking eggs. Weed watching him. The noise of the frying apart, silence.

The eggs are done. Slabb swallows two of them whole. They go down noisily.

Weed What is this, feeding time at the zoo?

Slabb We all have to eat, don't we?

Weed Call that eating?

Slabb If that whore of a sister of yours had ever taken time out of bed to learn to cook it would all be different.

Weed Are you talking of your wife?

Slabb What sort of wife is it that rubs her tits on every poor guy who happens to ask her what day of the week it is? I saw what went on last night. Do you think I'm blind?

Weed She's the wife you wanted her to be. She does it for you.

Slabb She does it for herself. Sometimes I make use of that fact, which I can't change.

Weed You made her that way.

Slabb She's always been a slag.

Weed Why'd you marry her then?

Slabb For her own good, if you must know...

Weed Jesus, that is the most incredible thing I've

ever heard anyone say about anything at all. Anywhere. In the whole history of mankind.

Slabb She was going nowhere. Fast.

Weed Nowhere was better than here with you.

Slabb When Brady was around?

Weed Brady didn't treat her like you do.

Slabb No. He'd have slit her throat years ago... That's enough of that talk.

Weed You don't talk to anyone. Unless it's abuse. Or orders. Mostly it's both.

Slabb I give you orders, you tosser, because without orders you don't know what to do with yourself. You'd sit on that bench in the middle of that rhododendron bush all day. Smoking yourself to death. Or else tossing off. You want to be in that infants' school, not sitting outside it. You might learn something.

Weed Jesus. Self satisfied or what? Big time.

Slabb You can't face up to the truth. I have to do it for you. Then I have to hold your hand and take you walkies through the garden...

Weed If it wasn't for Cathleen...

Slabb 'If it wasn't for Cathleen? If it wasn't for Cathleen?' If I hear that one more time I'll puke these eggs up all over you. Don't blame her. She's the one looking after you, not the other way around. Fuck sake, get with it. What have you ever done for Cathleen? Other than practically pull her skirt off while you were hanging on to it. Do you think I don't know you want to fuck with your own sister? I see the way you look at her.

Weed It takes a mind like yours to even think of that.

Slabb You think about it all the time. And you know what I mean by that.

Weed And what does Cathleen think about? Do you know? Have you ever stopped to think about that?

Weed pulls out the pack of Camels he has blagged off Fairfax, puts one between his lips. He tries to light it but drops the lighter. He says 'Fuck' and the cigarette falls out of his mouth onto the floor. Slabb watches this performance.

Slabb She knows where she'd be without me.

Weed *[finally lighting up]* Where's that?

Slabb On the street. Having a hard time, at her age. And with her looks, let's face it.

Weed Her looks? That's rich. Right now she's walking around with a black eye thanks to you. It's too dark to see out there and she's got to wear dark glasses.

Slabb Bruises heal.

Weed You animal.

Slabb She had it coming. It's between me and my wife.

Weed You hurt her, you animal.

Slabb She'll get over it. I know that. She knows it. And she knows I know it. But what you don't seem to know, Little Weed, is that there are ways I could hurt her much worse, much worse, so bad she'd never get over it.

Weed What are you talking about?

Slabb You just don't get it do you? You just don't get it.

Weed No. I don't.

Slabb Well maybe one day you will.

Weed One day. *[shakes his head 'pitifully']* One day. If you had any idea what, one day, she was looking forward to you'd...

Slabb I'd what?

Weed Nothing.

Slabb Well, what is she looking forward to?

Weed Freedom.

Slabb What, with you and Brady?

Weed With herself.

Slabb She knows that can't ever happen.

Weed Why?

Slabb Because she'll always have you traipsing around after her. All over the place. There's no freedom from you. She knows she can't get rid of you. I tell you, Weed, there's only one person who'll ever get rid of you. And that's Brady. You want to think about that.

Weed A saint, already? Jesus, you'll be applying for canonisation next. I bet you've already thought about it.

Slabb If I'm a saint I don't need to apply, do I? Think about it yourself.

15. White City

Thursday. Late afternoon. A church.

Dwarfed by the concrete pillars of the Westway is a small square church. Painted white it sits in the shadow of, on one side the motorway and, on the other, tall trees that flank an old graveyard.

Quinn pushes open the door of the church to see Cathleen sitting in the last pew. She is alone in the church. She is wearing dark glasses and a black plastic mac. She is slumped down in the pew with her hands deep in the pockets of her mac. She turns as he comes up to her.

Cathleen Did God send you?

Quinn No.

Cathleen How did you find me?

Quinn Weed said you could be here... Slabb's knocked you about?

Cathleen I thought these glasses hid it.

Quinn They do. Weed told me... I'm sorry.

Cathleen It's nothing. It was my fault.

Quinn What did you do, forget to sugar his tea?

Quinn sits beside her. Above the altar is a painted statue of Christ on the cross. Red paint indicates the blood on his hands and feet. It is strangely and powerfully realistic. Quinn can not help but stare at it. Cathleen watching him.

Cathleen Beautiful.

Quinn Yes.

Cathleen I come here when I know the place will be empty.

Quinn You come here a lot?

Cathleen It's empty a lot. I sit and stare. For hours.

Quinn Yes.

Cathleen The pain.

Quinn Yes.

Cathleen Why?

Quinn I don't know. *[pause]* Weed's on edge. I mean really.

Cathleen The shakes? He gets that way. Always has done. If something big is going to happen.

Quinn What is it he's worried about?

Cathleen I can't talk about this in here.

Quinn There's no-one to hear us.

Cathleen In a holy place you don't talk of sinning.

Quinn What sinning is that?

Cathleen The whole business is one big sin, isn't it?

Quinn What's Weed been saying?

Cathleen Nothing. Not to me.

Quinn Are you telling me the truth?

Cathleen Would I lie, in here?

Quinn Has he shown you the gun?

Cathleen Shh!

Quinn Has he?

Cathleen *[whispering]* Yes.

Quinn The gun makes him nervous, doesn't it?

Cathleen It does.

Quinn Why?

Cathleen He's like a child. I told you that before.

Quinn I didn't realise how much he hated Michael.

Cathleen Not hate... Emotion... Could even be love... Michael's the only one who's ever trusted him, given him something to do. Hamish can't take it. It tears him up. Michael's got too much power over him... He's not bad.

Quinn Angry then. Are you the same?

Cathleen I'm bad... God knows that.

She crosses herself.

Quinn You and Michael, will it last?

Cathleen You asked me that before.

Quinn I'm asking you again.

Cathleen He knows that too.

She crosses herself again.

Quinn But do you?

Cathleen I can't tell you.

Quinn Because you don't know?

Cathleen Because I can't tell you.

Quinn Tell me this then. Doctor Fairfax says Looby Loo's got to be at the meet. She's not there, no deal.

What do you know about her and the doctor?

Cathleen No more than anyone else.

Quinn How long have you known she was one of his patients?

Cathleen The first night she came in. He was in a corner, occupied shall we say, and didn't see her at first. She pointed him out to me and said did I know he was a doctor.

Quinn What did you say?

Cathleen The game's up then.

Quinn How long had he been using The Crypt when this happened?

Cathleen Months. I was still working for him, cleaning his rooms in Harley Street.

Quinn I'd like to know how long she's been one of his patients.

Cathleen Her seeing him there. Quite a coincidence.

16. Regent's Park

Thursday. 7pm. The Rolls-Royce.

Weed and Fairfax. Through the window, and in failing light, another load of women jumping around in short skirts in the tennis courts. Jesus, is that all they do?

Fairfax ...It has to be that way or I'm not in.

Weed And you know about me and Cathleen, and the gun?

Fairfax You didn't have to tell me.

Weed I had to. How else was I going to persuade you?

Fairfax It was your risk.

Weed It was that. Big time.

Fairfax I've thought about it. The risk to me the other way is too great. If he knows I'm carrying the report with me he can intercept me as soon as I'm on my way. He'd have his hands on it before I could get anywhere near him and I'd be back to square one without anything to bargain with. My way he can't touch me until I can touch him.

Weed A courier? What are you talking about, a motorbike delivery?

Fairfax Exactly. To The Crypt.

Weed When?

Fairfax Before I leave for The Crypt I deposit the document with a firm of couriers...

Weed Who are these people?

Fairfax Just couriers. The name of the firm I keep

to myself. They're completely reliable. I use them all the time. The report will be in an unmarked package. Before I leave I arrange for them to deliver the package to The Crypt at a given time. But, the bike will pull up half a mile away and wait for me to call from the phone in The Crypt. If anything is wrong when I get there, if Looby Loo isn't there, if Slabb isn't there, if anything at all is different from what we agreed I won't make the call. The rider will take the package back. Assuming I do make the call the rider proceeds to The Crypt where you, and only you, let him in. Slabb stays inside with me. The rider has strict instructions to hand over the package to me only.

Weed Slabb won't agree to that. Nor do I.

Fairfax Why not?

Weed How do we know what's in the package?

Fairfax I have to come in without it.

Weed Then it's stalemate. *[pause]* By the way...

Fairfax By the way what?

Weed Tell me about the report. What's in it?

Fairfax It's medical stuff Weed. A psychiatric report. It wouldn't mean anything to you.

Weed Tell me anyway. I want to hear you talk about it.

Fairfax Why?

Weed I want to know you're not lying. I want to know you've read it. Because to have read it you must have it.

Fairfax You don't trust me?

Weed No one trusts anyone do they?

Fairfax He's not well in his head, Weed. There's a serious problem with drink... He's a depressive schizophrenic, which means...

Weed Okay, okay. I get the picture. The Secretary's

on the juice. Sounds pretty normal...

PAUSE... before Fairfax resumes. He is looking out of the window, thinking as he speaks...

Fairfax Will Slabb be armed?

Weed He doesn't own a gun. You think he's scared of you?

Fairfax Alright... we'll do it like this. The bike comes to The Crypt on my call. He's been told that you will unseal and inspect the package at the door, but that he holds on to it and he himself hands it over to me. I have to protect myself against you running off with it yourself.

Weed Slabb should ok that.

Fairfax You want him dead. Get him to agree.

Weed He'll agree. He might wonder but he'll agree.

Fairfax Then we'll be in business. A bloody awful business. But we're not to blame are we? The one who's to blame is going to get punished. *[Weed stays silent]* The gun?

Weed hands the Woolworth bag between the seats. Fairfax keeps his hands inside the bag, releases the cylinder catch and swings out the cylinder. He checks the chambers are empty, pushes back the cylinder and tries the action through several complete turns of the cylinder.

Fairfax Well, that seems to work fine.

Weed There's four men in heaven who could swear to that.

Fairfax takes the red cardboard box from the bag- the black one has been removed- opens it, checks the cartridges, closes the box.

Fairfax All this is in order.

Weed You seem to know what you're doing, Doc. You haven't forgotten.

Fairfax You don't. Not when your life depends on it... It'll be in the cupboard under the sink?

Weed The yellow one. You remember it?

Fairfax Yes.

Weed It's full of junk. Cleaning stuff, mainly. Polish. Disinfectant. That kind of junk. Women's stuff. Slabb never looks in there, you can be sure of that. Even if he did he wouldn't look through a Woolworth bag. It's only what he'd expect to be there.

Fairfax So Slabb looks through the report then I ask to use the toilet. I come back with the gun... He can read, can he?

Weed Some words.

Fairfax Because if he can't he won't try reading it.

Weed He'll make out he's reading it. Just don't test him on it.

Fairfax I won't say anything at all to him.

Weed Then her, you've decided?

Fairfax I've no choice.

Weed Doing her won't be so easy.

Fairfax She hasn't spared me, has she?

Weed You said it.

Fairfax One thing worries me. It worries me a lot to tell you the truth.

Weed What?

Fairfax You loading the gun.

Weed Come on.

Fairfax You know how to do it?

Weed It's obvious isn't it?

Fairfax Well, it is... but...

Weed Load it yourself.

Fairfax Now?

Weed Why not?

Fairfax It can be dangerous. It is dangerous.

Weed I won't touch it. You load it. I won't take it out of the bag. The bag'll go straight into the cupboard under the sink Saturday evening. That way you'll be sure it's all ready to go.

Fairfax I think I will.

Fairfax keeps his hands inside the bag, loads the gun, hands the Woolworth bag back to Weed.

...It's done. Put it somewhere safe, Weed. I mean it. Don't get it out to have a look at it. You might just find you've solved all your problems in one go.

Weed Jesus.

Fairfax Now I want you to tell me something... Has Slabb ever talked to you about King's Cross?

Weed The train station?

Fairfax Not the station. The area.

Weed What about it?

Fairfax He hasn't then?

Weed No... The area, what do you mean?

Fairfax Never?

Weed Never. Why?

Fairfax Something happened there. Looby Loo mentioned it. Yesterday. She's never spoken about it before. I wondered what she knew, who told her. I wondered if Slabb knew...

Weed Never heard talk of it. What happened there?

Fairfax If you don't know it's best we keep it that way. It's got nothing to do with Saturday. Look, do we meet again?

Weed No need. Unless something comes up.

Fairfax Saturday afternoon perhaps? So I know it's still on.

Weed What time?

Fairfax Three? Bring the gun with you.

Weed Three then.

Fairfax You're not taking that on the bus, are you?

Weed Better give me cab fare.

17. Sands End

Midnight , Thursday.

Heavy rain. A street empty of people. Houses boarded up.

Sitting in the rented Ford Quinn takes a slug of whisky from a small bottle of Bells, returns it to his jacket pocket. He is parked down from the house where Helen Suter has a first floor room. There is no light in the house but the street door is open, as it has been all the time Quinn has been waiting there.

Twice in two hours a motorcycle has stopped at the junction with the nearest cross street while the rider looked down towards the house. Now the motorbike, a high cc Kawasaki, turns into the street, cruises slowly past the house. At the end of the street it turns and passes back by the house before leaving by the cross street.

Quinn gets out of the Ford. As the bike made its turn he has noticed something caught for a moment in its headlight; something gleaming in the rain. He walks past Helen's room and stops at the gate of a boarded up house further down the street. Helen Suter, in her leather suit and boots, is curled up among the bins, asleep in the rain. Her handbag is open on the ground beside her. She is clutching a half bottle of Johnny Walker which she has either drunk or emptied on to herself as she fell asleep.

Quinn shakes her half awake, lifts her off the ground by the snakehead buckle of her belt and walks/drags her up the street to her own house and up the stairs to her room. As he is doing this she mumbles, half sings 'Drinky...little drinky...one little drinky...', whether to herself or Quinn isn't clear.

Quinn lays her on her back on the bed, finds the bathroom and comes back with a towel. He takes off her waistcoat and towels off her naked upper body. He tries to towel her hair and face. Doing this brings her out of her sleep. She opens her eyes and splutters, still heavily sedated.

Helen Drinky sir, kind sir... little drinky?... Please?

Quinn Go to sleep.

Helen One little drinky... just one?..Go on, sir.

Quinn I don't have any.

Helen But you do, kind sir... in your pocket... one little one?

Quinn lifts her head and holds her up by the shoulders. He unscrews the bottle of Bells and gives it to her. She downs what is left in two swallows, drops the empty bottle on the floor and collapses onto her back giggling.

Helen [continued] Kind sir... I've been expecting you.

Quinn You know who I am?

Helen Oh yes... definitely.

Quinn How?

Helen ...Spies...

Quinn Slabb and Weed?

Helen Slabb and Weed... My heroes.

Quinn They said they hadn't seen you for days.

Helen *[still giggling]* Ah... well, you can't believe everything you read in the newspapers, can you?

Quinn Helen...

Helen Looby Loo.

Quinn Your trousers and boots are soaking. You have to take them off.

Helen You sir... you do it... you.

Quinn Are you sure?

Helen *[eyes half closing]* ...You...

Quinn unzips her boots and pulls them off. There are holes in the toes and soles, the heels near breaking off. He unclasps the snakehead buckle of her belt, unzips her trousers and pulls them off. They are so tight that her panties come off with them. She stirs, laughs, '...kind sir...' He takes the boots and trousers and puts them in the bathroom to dry. When he comes back she is asleep. He pulls a blanket over her and sits in a beaten up armchair opposite the end of the bed. He watches her sleeping for some time before the gentle sound of her snoring sends him off.

Morning.

Quinn wakes to see her sitting on the bed facing him. She has washed and 'dressed' while he slept. Her 'dress' is a pair of tight bikini panties together with the belt with the snakehead buckle. She is sitting with her knees up, her back against the wall at the head of the bed. She is smoking a cigarette, a saucer on the pillow as her ashtray.

Helen Good morning.

Quinn *[rubbing his eyes]* Just what I was thinking.

Helen I thought you'd never wake.

Quinn I am awake, am I?... What the hell are you made of?

Helen Strong stuff... Quinn, isn't it?

Quinn Yes.

Helen Nice name.

Quinn Thanks.

Helen Just as well. You're not much to look at. In fact, you're a big disappointment.

Quinn Thanks again.

Helen Do you know my type, the sort of man I really go for? Tall, slim, shoulder length black curls.*[she draws in the air with her cigarette]* And young.

Quinn I'm so happy for you.

Helen I was just thinking, looking at you there in the chair, that if I saw you in the street I wouldn't even see you.

Quinn Well, I'd like to be able to say the same about you. But...

Helen ...You do have charisma.

Quinn Not much use if people can't even see me.

Helen Thanks for last night.

Quinn Is that where you normally sleep, someone else's garden?

Helen I try to get the right house.

Quinn It was dark, right?

Helen You're a gentleman.

Quinn Someone else said that. Who was it?... Anyway, you know who I am. Do you know why I'm here?

Helen I think so.

Quinn You've got a date Saturday night. The Crypt. Ten o'clock.

Helen Ten?

Quinn You didn't know the time?

Helen I wasn't told the time.

Quinn Ten o'clock. Unless something changes.

Helen Okay.

Quinn You know what's going to happen?

Helen I hear the doctor's finally going to produce the rabbit out of his hat... Magic.

She stubs out in the saucer, lights another cigarette.

Quinn What do you get out of it?

Helen You'd like to know wouldn't you?

Quinn Won't say?

Helen Can't.

Quinn You're afraid to?

Helen I'm not a total wreck. I've got one or two cells left. When I can find them.

Quinn You're not a wreck at all. Far from it.

Helen Gentleman.

Quinn What's your idea about Slabb?

Helen What about him?

Quinn What do you know about him?

Helen You're trying to trick me, I think.

Quinn Okay, leave it. By the way, I love the belt. What is it?

Helen Take a look.

Helen unbuckles the belt, holds it out. Quinn gets up from the chair, takes it and sits down again to examine it.

Quinn Heavy.

Helen Bronze, baby.

Quinn How do you wear that all day?

Helen Love.

Quinn An admirer?

Helen Hardly. My brother. My long lost brother.

Quinn What is it, African or something?

Helen Something... Native. That sort of thing. You know.

Quinn Sounds about right... 'Your long lost brother'? Aren't you the one that's long lost?

Helen One of us is.

Quinn Where's he gone, on safari and never coming back?

Helen Exactly.

Quinn Where?

Helen Big game hunting.

Quinn But where?

Helen Right here. In London. *[she laughs]*

Quinn You're crazy.

Helen You should see him.

Quinn What does he do?

Helen Lunch, mainly.

Quinn That's it?

Helen Oui, c'est tout, cheri. Lunch. With his

cronies.

Quinn Who they?

Helen You've heard of The Wild Bunch?

Quinn Yes.

Helen Not them. This is the bunch of bananas. The original ones. Politics, politics, politics. You know, how do we stop people getting their hands on our money?

Quinn This is the brother that lives at Eaton Place?

Helen Ah. Perhaps I've said too much. Or anyway, it seems you know too much.

Quinn Why?

Helen If I told you that I really would have said too much.

Quinn Here's something you can tell me. How long have you been one of the doctor's patients?

Helen Can I tell you that? ...Perhaps I can. Let's see... six months I should say.

Quinn Who arranged it?

Helen My long lost brother.

Quinn The one who's big game hunting?

Helen The same. A birthday present, I think.

Quinn What's Doctor Fairfax treating you for? Can I ask?

Helen Heartache, darling.

Quinn Is that all?

Helen Isn't it enough?

Quinn I'm serious, Helen.

Helen I'm serious too, Quinn. Very.

Quinn I'd say the doctor was regretting taking you on.

Helen His bills are paid.

Quinn By your brother?

Helen Not by me.

Quinn Why are you doing this to him?

Helen Why does anyone do anything?

Quinn Money? You don't seem the type.

Helen Don't be nosey. I was beginning to like you. I pay my way. One way or another. Cigarette?

Quinn Thanks.

Helen chucks a cigarette at Quinn. It hits him in the face. He lights up.

Helen Coffee?

Quinn If it's on.

Helen slings her legs off the bed and stands up. She straightens her panties back and front, smiles at him.

Helen Don't go away now.

Quinn Swear to God.

She leaves the room, comes back with two cups of coffee, gives Quinn his and climbs back on the bed.

Quinn [continued] ...Who took the photos? You?

Helen Kidding? He wouldn't have let me take pictures of him in there.

Quinn That's what I thought. Who then?

Helen They'd already been taken before I started going there.

Quinn You mean before anyone at the club knew who he was?

Helen Slabb knew.

Quinn You're right. I forgot. Slabb knew.

Helen They're just party photos, Quinn.

Quinn And Fairfax just happened to figure in all of them?

Helen He puts himself about. Believe me. When he's in the right company.

Quinn What are they like?

Helen Him groping a load of good time grannies. Head or hands up their skirts. Cock too when he can manage it, which isn't often.

Quinn Who's got them?

Helen Slabb.

Quinn The negatives?

Helen Slabb.

Quinn Somebody handed all their party photos over to Slabb? Why would they do that?

Helen He can be quite frightening.

Quinn Unless Slabb took them himself, or got someone to take them. But I thought it was your idea to screw the doctor... Was it?

PAUSE

Helen Whose side are you on Quinn?

Quinn My own. Whose side are you on?

Helen I'm like you.

Quinn Maybe we should team up.

Helen I'd like to. Charisma.

Quinn Slabb's place, The Crypt. How come you went there? Who took you?

Helen I end up in a lot of places, Quinn. With a lot of people. What you've got to remember... is that given my... what shall I call it?... I don't want to be too hard on myself...

Quinn Weakness?

Helen Exactly. Given my little weakness, I don't always know everything about where I've been.

Quinn You don't remember?

Helen I think that's what I was trying to say.

Quinn Nice coffee.

Helen There's more. Plenty more.

Quinn No... more... you know... Helen?

Helen Quinn?...

Quinn Last night... You said you knew I was coming...

Helen If I said that I shouldn't have.

Quinn How did you know?

Helen Intuition?

Quinn Your brother?

Helen How could he know?

Quinn Yes, how could he?... It's funny... Helen... You're the only one who hasn't asked me who I am and what I'm doing here.

Helen I don't care who you are.

Quinn Or you know already.

Helen If I did know I still wouldn't care... Do you smoke at all, Quinn?

Quinn No.

Helen Shame. I feel like one.

Quinn Don't let me stop you.

Helen You're going?

Quinn I guess.

She lets her knees fall apart then quickly snaps them together.

Helen Wouldn't you like some breakfast, something to eat?

Quinn I'm not hungry.

Helen A little bite perhaps?

Quinn Well...

Helen Go on.

Her knees fall apart again and her hand slips between her thighs. She slowly brings her hand up over her panties to her abdomen.

...You can't go all day on an empty stomach, Quinn. I know I can't. It's very bad for you, they say.

Quinn A quick taste maybe.

Helen That's what I like to hear.

Quinn You try hard to be, but you're not what you seem are you?

Helen *[shrugs]* Who is? It's all an illusion, isn't it?
Quinn What is?
Helen It, of course.

Quinn stands over her as she lays down on the bed.

Quinn Take care of yourself, Helen. You know no-one else is going to.

Helen I'll be fine. Now come here.

18. White City

Friday am. The kitchen of the Slabb flat.

The table shows the remains of breakfast, which has been eaten in silence.

Outside the sound of a horse and cart, now and then a bell being rung. Any old iron?

Slabb Two days.

Weed Till Brady?

Slabb Shit.

Weed One day. Jesus.

Slabb Till tomorrow?

Weed Jesus.

Slabb Not enough time. Shit.

Weed Jesus, I don't know which is worse.

Slabb I do. Shit.

Cathleen Even if he comes, he's no reason to take it out on you.

Slabb He can take it out on anyone he feels like. When did he ever need a reason?

Weed Well if he did need one you've given it to him.

Slabb By looking after Cathleen?

Weed Been keeping her nice?

Slabb I've been keeping her, which is more than he'd have ever done.

Weed Let's face it. Brady's got it in for you. I don't

blame him.

Cathleen You don't know that.

Slabb Well, let me tell you something, you two.

Weed Yeah, what?

Slabb Suppose he's got it in for you? And for Cathleen too?

Cathleen Me? What have I done?

Slabb Left him for me didn't you? You only dumped him.

Cathleen It wasn't like that. He knows that.

Slabb No, maybe not. But he's been inside. Being locked up for years can do funny things to a man's brain. And his brain was worse than funny long before he went in. Who knows what's been preying on his mind night after night?

Cathleen ...Nothing to do with me.

Slabb Could be he blames you for everything that's happened to him since you came with me. Some men are like that. Maybe he's thinking if she hadn't turned me down maybe I'd never have gone bad and been locked up and now I can never go home. And it's all her fault. All she had to do was say yes to me. You know how some people think.

Weed What are you trying to do, scare my sister?

Slabb Brady's crazy. Who knows what he's thinking? It could be anything. And if he's thinking what I just said, well, Cathleen better look out.

Weed Shut up trying to scare her I said.

Cathleen I'm not scared. I know Donal Brady. And he would have kept me.

Slabb You knew him you mean. You too, Weed. For all you know you may be his number one target.

Weed Trying to scare me too?

Slabb It's not difficult.

Weed You're gonna get a big scare yourself soon, Michael. Believe me. A big surprise.

Slabb You're going to turn out to be a hero? That would be a big surprise. It could even be scary. But I won't be holding my breath.

Weed You wait.

Slabb Till when?

Weed Not long.

Slabb It wouldn't be till Brady gets here, by any chance? You make me laugh. You think you're gonna make it up with him like some long lost brother, don't you? You are the prodigal you know what, do you know that?

Weed Yeah, the prodigal what?

Slabb Asshole. You are the prodigal asshole. Your eyes are so full of shit you can't see past your own ring. You can't see what's just beyond your own ring waiting to be shoved up it. You and Brady and Cathleen happy ever after? Make your will, Weed, because you could be the one who's throat he slits first. Just to check whether the knife is still sharp.

Weed Why would he start on me when there's a dog turd like you around?

Slabb Don't you know? Well, I'll tell you. Because you're weak, Weed, like an insect. You're like a sick stick insect with a broken leg. You crawl round and round in circles because you can't help it. And people watch you going nowhere and then nowhere and then nowhere until it drives you crazy. At first they laugh but in the end people get sick of watching it. You make them feel sick themselves. You're just the sort of thing some people, people like Brady, like to stamp on. Or maybe he'll just pull your legs and other bits off. He'll be laughing while he does it, watching you wriggle and writhe and try to move without any legs until finally you just stop moving and die. In pain.

Weed You bastard.

Slabb I'll tell you something else. Brady might not have it in for me at all. He might be saying 'What chance did he have, saddled with a no good tramp and a cross between a halfwit stick insect and a leech for a family?' The poor man, I bet he's thinking, I'll do him a favour and do what he never had the heart to do for himself. I'll lighten his load.

Weed You've lost it. Big time.

Cathleen Call us your load?

Slabb Isn't that what you are, what you've been, the pair of you? How many men would have carried that load, and willingly, when they didn't have to? Tell me that.

Cathleen You loved me.

Slabb I did too. I do. So?

Cathleen So I was no load, was I?

Slabb You were heavy. And you came with baggage.

Cathleen I could say the same about you.

Slabb Well isn't that how it's meant to be?

Weed Jesus. You're mad. Big time. As bad as Brady. *[to Cathleen]* Come on, Sis, let's go out. Why listen to any more of this? Soon we won't have to.

Slabb Plotting?

Weed Who's plotting?

Slabb That's what I'm asking you.

Weed What have you got into your head now?

Slabb I'm asking you two if you're plotting. It's plain English isn't it?

Weed Plotting what, for God's sake?

Slabb If I knew that I wouldn't be asking you would I?

Weed *[standing up]* Jesus. Mad house. Big time. I'm outa here...

Slabb Yeah, tell me something new... Where's that gun?

Weed In the bag, where it's supposed to be.

Slabb Fetch it.

Weed fetches the Woolworth bag from another room, hands it to Slabb.

Weed The Doc's loaded it already.

Slabb Didn't trust you to do it right? He's a good judge, if nothing else. We need to unload this. Quick. Or else I might not be needing that document. Reload the dummies. I want to see you do it.

Slabb gives the Colt back to Weed. Weed works the cylinder catch, swings open the cylinder. He tips the gun up and empties the live cartridges into the palm of his hand. He puts them into the red box. He opens the black box and from it loads the dummy rounds into the chambers. He pushes the cylinder back in place.

Weed That's it.

Slabb Pretty good. You been practising?

Weed Quinn's showed me how.

Slabb The live ammo...

Weed I keep it. Quinn says.

Slabb Does he now? And why, I ask myself.

Weed It stays with the gun. What if The Doc asks to see the gun one more time? I'll have to reload the live bullets to show him then reload the dummies after he's seen it... It's easy enough.

Slabb Seems like any fool can do it.

19. White City

Friday pm. A graveyard.

Quinn finds Cathleen sitting on a bench in the graveyard beside the white church. Beyond one wall of the graveyard a dark, grimy, almost black brick building. It is a children's hospital. As he comes up to her he can hear her mumbling to herself as she scratches at a nearby gravestone with a stick. It is raining steadily.

Quinn Why are you out here in the rain? The church is empty.

Cathleen I can never go in there again. I'm no longer welcome in His house.

Quinn sits beside her. They speak for several minutes. Their conversation is animated. As they speak the rain penetrates the canopy of pine branches above them and falls on them in big droplets. Soon Cathleen picks up the twig she has been using to scratch at the gravestone and starts turning it in her fingers.

Cathleen Sweet Mary, who will forgive me?

Quinn You don't need forgiving.

Cathleen What have I done? What am I doing? What is it I am about to do?

Quinn You're saving your brother aren't you? And saving yourself?

Cathleen Saving? What do you know of salvation?

Quinn I know when it's needed. What has he done to you? Anyone that's not blind can see it.

Cathleen Haven't I sinned enough? And now I'm to sin against the man I'm sworn to.

Quinn Who was it that caused you to sin all these years?

Cathleen Me. It's been me. I'm bad through. Can't you see? Every inch of me is bad. Look at me. Can't you tell?

Quinn Tell the truth Cathleen. You married the devil.

Cathleen You put this on a poor fallen woman?

She leans forward, scratches again at the gravestone, digging the moss out of the lettering at its top. Begins to read aloud...

...Sacred to the memory... *[skips to the end.]* ...Died aged two. Poor soldier. What chance did he have?

Quinn None. Unlike you.

Cathleen The little girl in the next grave. Dead at eighteen months. Dear God, the infants...

Quinn Cathleen, you're still living.

Cathleen If I am I don't deserve to be *[waves at the children's hospital]*. The little ones in there, Quinn. Why do they have to die? Of all people, why them?

Quinn Who knows?

Cathleen There's no sense in it.

Quinn There's no sense in any of it. Don't try to find any. Take your chance. Don't question why you've been given one.

Cathleen How noble.

Quinn You never had children?

Cathleen No little ones.

Quinn Why was that? Do you mind me asking?

Cathleen I don't mind anything.

Quinn Didn't he want any?

Cathleen Can't have done can he? Not by me anyway.

Quinn Didn't you want kids?

Cathleen I wanted all sorts of things. When I was young.

Quinn And what do you want now?

Cathleen turns to scratching at the gravestone again.

Cathleen To do the right thing. That's all... Sacred to the memory... Will my memory be sacred, Quinn?... Answer me that.

Quinn More than most, I'd say.

Cathleen How so?

Quinn You've suffered.

Cathleen I brought it on myself.

Quinn I don't think so. Those who know won't think so.

Cathleen stops scratching, listens to the church clock sound the hour.

Cathleen Five. Betrayal. Can it have come to this?

Quinn You can be free. You and your brother.

Cathleen Treachery. The worst sin of all. Worse than all my other sins. The man I'm married to. Betray God. Sweet Mary, help me.

Quinn And what of your brother? Look at him. What has Michael done to him?

Cathleen My brother's not my responsibility. That's not my duty.

Quinn He's doing it for you, Cathleen. You know that. He at least can face the truth. So must you.

Cathleen Betrayal. Treachery. Mary.

Quinn If you don't you betray yourself.

Cathleen That's no sin.

Quinn Isn't it?

Cathleen indicates the headstone with the twig.

Cathleen And who'll look after my grave, Quinn? Will it be like this one? Will someone sit and scratch the moss out of my name and then think nothing of it, like this poor child?

Quinn Cathleen, how do I know?

Cathleen There'll be no-one. No-one to tend my grave. No-one to lay fresh flowers.

Quinn You'll find someone. Maybe Brady, who knows?

Cathleen There'll be no-one. I know it. My grave will be a mess. They'll have to burn me.

Quinn What difference?

Cathleen I wanted to rest in a nice shady spot. I wanted to go to heaven, Quinn.

Quinn You'll go to heaven.

Cathleen I may have to burn.

20. White City

Friday pm. The bench.

Twilight. Quinn and Weed. No sounds from the school. Bedrolls and cardboard boxes, homemade bivouacs, materialise in the gloom.

Quinn Seen Looby Loo?

Weed She's scarpered. You've seen her?

Quinn Maybe you had too.

Weed No sign.

Quinn Slabb?

Weed Would I know?

Quinn He wouldn't tell you?

Weed How would I know?

Quinn What does he tell you?

Weed About what?

Quinn Blackmailing The Doc, for one. Forcing him to steal information that could be passed to the press? Whose idea was that?

Weed We got instructions, Slabb said.

Quinn Slabb said. Instructions from where?

Weed Ireland, where else?

Quinn Where else?... When are you seeing The Doc?

Weed Tomorrow. Three.

Quinn The love letters... You made that up yourself?

Weed Did I do wrong?

Quinn Nice touch.

Weed The bit I like best is Brady not being able to write. Having to get someone else to write his love letters.

Quinn He can write?

Weed You said it. Teacher's pet. Top of the form. In everything. Drove the rest of us sick.

Quinn And you were second top. Am I right?

Weed Well, I was.

Quinn In everything?

Weed Not sport.

Quinn Not sport... When you've seen The Doc I want you to tell Slabb something. But only after you've seen The Doc.

Weed Tell Slabb what?

Quinn The Doc's told you something about the report, what's in it.

Weed He's already told me.

Quinn Not what I'm going to tell you.

Weed Don't you want to know what he told me?

Quinn I'm telling you what to tell Slabb.

Weed Aren't you interested in what's in the report? I don't get this.

Quinn This is about what you are going to say is in the report.

Weed Even if The Doc said nothing about it?

Quinn Even if he has. You tell Slabb anyway.

Weed Why?

Quinn I want to see what Slabb does when you tell him.

Weed Why?

Quinn I've got my reasons.

Weed And I don't need to know?

Quinn No.

Weed Why?

Quinn Why what?

Weed Don't I need to know.

Quinn It could be nothing.

Weed Well, okay... For now... What do I tell Slabb?

Quinn The Secretary of State's sick, right? That's why there is a report. But he's not just sick, he's paranoid...

Weed Paranoid?

Quinn Conspiracies. They're everywhere. He can't trust anyone. No one. People want him out. Not just Republicans, Unionists too. Especially Unionists. Things are being arranged behind his back. In London, as well as Dublin and Belfast. Now the Secretary's set up a team of agents who report to him only. These agents are watching men who are supposed to be on his own side, civil servants in London, people in The Ministry of Defence.

Weed Is it true?

Quinn Which part?

Weed Any part.

Quinn It could be.

Weed You invented it.

Quinn It's a possibility. Which is why you don't need to think about it. Why worry over a load of lies? But let's see whether Slabb does, okay?

Weed Okay. I'll tell him. If you want... Now I gotta tell you something. You want this document as bad as Slabb, you have to deliver right?

Quinn And?

Weed Slabb doesn't trust you. You can't have a weapon in there tomorrow. He's gonna frisk you. You're tooled up and it's all off. He's going to pull the plug. Fuck the whole thing... Fuck you, fuck The Doc. Fuck the report, fuck Brady fuck Cathleen and fuck me. Trafalgar can go fuck too... You have to be clean, Quinn.

Quinn That Slabb's idea or did it come from Trafalgar?

Weed This Trafalgar, he doesn't give you his own messages?

Quinn He does what suits him... ok, so this is Slabb. Why?

Weed Something's up, he says. Can't trust anyone. Especially not you and that boss of yours.

Quinn Losing it then.

Weed He lost it years ago.

Quinn That's the way it is, that's how it will have to be. *[pause]* Don't forget that story I told you.

Weed Here's another one. Maybe. Unless it's one of yours. What's this about King's Cross?

Quinn The train station? What about it?

Weed *[laughs]* Just what I said myself. What are you on about I said?... Anyway, not the station. The area. The Doc said did me or Slabb know about it. Something happened there.

Quinn What happens in King's Cross is public knowledge. What happened to The Doc there?

Weed Wouldn't say.

Quinn When then?

Weed Wouldn't say neither. Only, somehow, Looby Loo knows about it and he can't figure out how. Is this something else you made up?

Quinn Don't worry about this.

Weed Who's worrying?

21. Sands End

Friday 10pm. Helen Suter's bedroom.

Light from a streetlight enters through the uncurtained window.

On the bed Helen Suter turns her head to see the silhouette of a large man in the doorway.

>**Helen** What are you doing here?
>
>**Fairfax** We need to talk.
>
>**Helen** Cigarette... Water.

Fairfax leaves the room, turns on a light in the kitchen and finds a glass. He turns out the light and comes back. She swallows the water in one.

>**Helen** Smoke.

Fairfax takes out a packet of Camels, offers it to her. She takes one and he lights it. He sits down on the end of the bed, lights up himself.

>**Fairfax** Helen...
>
>**Helen** How?...
>
>**Fairfax** Private detective.
>
>**Helen** Followed me home?
>
>**Fairfax** Yes.
>
>**Helen** From Harley Street?

Fairfax Via Eaton Place. More than once.

Helen Oh well.

Fairfax What were you doing there?

Helen It's my home.

Fairfax Isn't this your home?

Helen The family home. My brother's home.

Fairfax That's what I mean.

Helen I can visit my brother.

Fairfax Helen. Please listen.

Helen Headache... Drink.

Fairfax goes out, comes back with a tumbler of whisky. She puts her finger in it, licks it off, then takes a swig.

Fairfax We've been set up.

Helen No bedtime stories. Too late.

Fairfax You and Slabb. Your relationship. I don't believe in it.

Helen I don't have a relationship with Slabb.

Fairfax This sordid deal, supposedly between you and him, to blackmail me.

Helen It's happening, I would have said.

Fairfax From the beginning it didn't make sense. Why were you doing this to me? What had I done to deserve it?... You said Slabb forced you. But what did Slabb have over you? And anyway how had Slabb managed to put all this together? I couldn't understand.

Helen And now you do? Understand?

Fairfax Everything that seemed to be obvious, had I thought about it, in fact wasn't. This whole thing has been planned. But not by Slabb. My cleaning woman, who'd been with me for years, suddenly disappearing. Slabb's wife turning up to take her place. The photos. All taken long before you showed up... You signing up as one of my patients, all bills paid by your brother... There's nothing wrong with you... there never has been.

Helen A matter of opinion, might you allow?

Fairfax Not medical opinion. The information I've been forced to steal. You take it to Eaton Place. Slabb never sees it, I would wager. The fact is, Helen, you are just the delivery boy.

Helen Some imagination. Or perhaps I should say who's feeding you your ideas?

Fairfax Someone is feeding you yours. And everyone else's as well. Isn't that the truth?

Helen If we knew what the truth was, any of us, life would be simple. But we don't do we? And it sure as hell isn't.

Fairfax I could find out... With your help.

Helen Tomorrow... it's over.

Fairfax Is it? How do I know who else is behind all this, who else knows?

Helen I suppose you have to take a chance.

Fairfax How do I know how many there are, photos or negatives? Do you know?... What about copies?

Helen I don't know of copies.

Fairfax He could have made some without telling you. Other people may have copies.

Helen Of course.

Fairfax Then what's the point of all this for me? It could all start again next week. Or next month. Or in five years. It won't be over until I'm dead.

Helen Or until you don't give a damn. Which in your case is when you're dead. You have to go with this because for you it's all there is.

Fairfax Can you help?

Helen No. I can't.

Fairfax We all have weaknesses. Even you.

Helen You could have been a cab driver. You could have fucked every old hag in London and none of it would matter. You chose differently. You wanted your cake and eat it.

Fairfax Only someone born into money could say that.

Helen If you can see that much then you need to take more care not to make wrong choices.

Fairfax Know all about me, don't you?

Helen Enough.

Fairfax King's Cross. You know what happened there. It all took place months before I ever met you. Nothing was ever published about it anywhere and I know for a fact that I have never spoken to anyone about it. Who told you Helen?

Helen What did happen there? Why don't you tell me?

Fairfax Vice. As you well know. Someone tipped them off. Or maybe I was unlucky.

Helen You do seem to be unlucky. Arrested?

Fairfax Let off with a warning. So I thought... What I asked you was how did you find out?

Helen That I can't remember.

Fairfax You can't say?

Helen If I can't remember I can't say.

PAUSE

Fairfax Pointless... Listen, I don't know what you know. I don't know what you don't know. I don't even know what I know or don't know myself. I only know I'm tired.

Helen You're going to go through with it?

Fairfax What else can I do?

Helen Alec... get the bottle.

Fairfax goes to the kitchen, comes back with a glass and the bottle. He tops her up, pours himself a glass. They clink glasses.

Fairfax I tried.

Helen Too hard.

Fairfax We could have been, should have been, friends.

Helen We've got different things in our heads, you and me.

Fairfax Maybe.

Helen Definitely.

Fairfax How tired are you?

Helen Enough.

Fairfax Can I stay?

Helen I don't know about stay.

Fairfax For a while?

Helen Can you handle it?

Fairfax You know I can.

Helen With me, I mean.

Fairfax Give me a chance.

Helen One chance. Then you let me sleep.

Fairfax lies on top of her. But she doesn't seem to care one way or the other. There is nothing. She begins to doze as he is trying. In a minute she wakes and pushes him off her.

Helen I knew nothing would happen, Doctor. You should have known it yourself.

Fairfax *[standing up, zipping his trousers)* Really? And Why?

Helen You need your women inferior to you. That's the only way you can get it up. We've all got our own poisons, Doctor. Slabb's old hags are yours. The older and uglier the more you turn on. Trouble is, Doctor, you know I'm not inferior to you. Not in any way, shape or form.

Fairfax Goodbye, Helen.

Helen *[blows him a kiss]* Au revoir.

22. White City

Saturday am. Slabb's tin hut.

A bright, very windy morning. Quinn and Slabb opposite each other in the dark of the hut. Quinn looks out at the street. A page of newspaper dancing on the gusts of wind. It floats across the bright screen, disappears from view out of one edge. A moment later it reappears from a different angle. The picture of a naked girl. The smell of Slabb's clothing.

Slabb What are you going to do about it?

Quinn It's not my problem.

Slabb I'll make it yours.

Quinn What good will that do?

Slabb It might save my life. They're plotting.

Quinn They're always plotting.

Slabb This is different.

Quinn Plotting to kill you?

Slabb Wouldn't be beyond them.

Quinn Way beyond them.

Slabb Cathleen's had word from Brady maybe. Maybe he's in on it. Maybe Weed has. How do I know?

Quinn Until you do know what can anyone do?

Slabb You won't do something, I will.

Quinn How can you do anything till you know what they intend to do? Find that out first. When are they going to do it. How.

Slabb There's a gun.

Quinn Tonight, at the meet? With The Doc there?

Slabb Good a time as any.

Quinn A gun loaded with dummy rounds that's going to be hidden in the cupboard under the sink? How is that a threat?

Slabb They're plotting. I know.

Quinn Well, how do you know?

Slabb Gone quiet... Usually they argue all the time. With me, with each other. It's all gone quiet.

Quinn Don't lose it now, Slabb.

Slabb Look, I want out of this. I'm sick of the whole thing. I just want that report. Then I want out.

Quinn Out... of what?

Slabb This shit.

Quinn It's all there is. You want that report, you've got to eat it. You want out, really, then let Brady come. Let him get the report.

Slabb I said I wanted out. Not cut to into strips by that butcher.

Quinn What's into you?

Slabb The lot of them. The Doc. He makes me puke. He fucks my wife on his consulting couch every day for six months then plans to kill her. What kind of man is that?... Looby Loo. I tell you I never want to see that bit of cunt again. Nor any bit of cunt. A man can get sick of cunt, did you know that Quinn?

Quinn I was two years without it.

Slabb Inside?

Quinn A blag. One that blew up.

Slabb Meaning?

Quinn Someone shot me.

Slabb Who?

Quinn I mean to find out.

Slabb They got away and you did time?

Quinn I was meant to be dead.

Slabb Two years, for a blag? Was the judge one of your uncles?

Quinn I did two years is what I said.

Slabb You got out? When was this?

Quinn Not long.

Slabb You're on the run and you work for Trafalgar? What the fuck is this?

Quinn There's a way. Think about it.

Slabb Don't have the time. This is about that piece of paper. Nothing else. I get that, Brady stays where he is and I stay alive. Then I'm out. For good.

Quinn That's not how Trafalgar sees it. This is about keeping you where he wants you.

Slabb Does Trafalgar run my life?

Quinn More than you think perhaps... Remember what I said. He's watching. Rooftops. High windows. Parked cars. You'll never see anyone but they're there. Every move. Step out of line, you or me, he'll act.

Slabb Then he does run my life.

Quinn I need that report too Slabb. As much as you. There's nowhere to run. Not for you not for me. Everyday you're still alive is one more. Until it's over. Don't fuck up on this.

Slabb And give Brady an excuse?... No, I'm good.

Quinn Stay with it.

Slabb It's there... I just can't see it.

They come out of the hut, stand in the wind, listen to the cries of the market traders. Slabb offers his hand. Quinn takes it.

Quinn When did you last see Looby Loo?

Slabb Not for days. A week maybe. Not since you arrived anyway.

Quinn Sure?

Slabb Of course I'm sure.

Quinn You okay with this thing about the courier, delivering the document after Fairfax has arrived?

Slabb Whatever. What difference can it make? I could trust, you could I?

Quinn On what?

Slabb Tell me if you find anything out.

Quinn Weed and Cathleen?

Slabb Anything.

Quinn Of course. I need this thing to go off the way it's planned.

Slabb I guess.

Quinn There's no way for them to do it.

Slabb The Doc could do it for them.

Quinn With a gun loaded with dummy rounds?

Slabb How will I be sure that it is?

Quinn Easy enough. Check the gun yourself at the last minute, just before Weed plants it. Take the live rounds off him and stick them in your pocket.

23. White City

Saturday am. The kitchen of the Slabb flat.

Coming up through the open window the strains of an argument in the street over the quality of something ... what?... just purchased at a knockdown price.

> **Weed** Give us the sugar.
>
> **Cathleen** Sweet enough aren't you?

Cathleen pushes the sugar bowl across the table, watches him dump three lumps into his mug of tea, stir noisily.

> ...I don't like it.
>
> **Weed** I'm not saying I like it. There's no other way. I'm his slave. We're both his slaves.
>
> **Cathleen** You could have left. Any time.
>
> **Weed** And left you with him?
>
> **Cathleen** So you blame me?
>
> **Weed** You're trapped. Same as me.
>
> **Cathleen** I've been a good wife.
>
> **Weed** Better by far than he deserved.
>
> **Cathleen** I've made his bed. I've washed and ironed. He's not wanted on my account.
>
> **Weed** It's true. If I could've ever had a woman she'd have had to be like you, Cathleen.
>
> **Cathleen** Why?...
>
> **Weed** I mean it.

Cathleen Wouldn't it be good to just start over?

Weed Back to school, eh?

Cathleen Back to school.

Weed You always were too good for him.

Cathleen There's many men have told me so. Have asked me to go wash and cook for them.

Weed I don't doubt it.

Cathleen I know I've sinned.

Weed Well...

Cathleen I've been the woman he wanted. That's what a good wife is, isn't it?

Weed What else?

Cathleen Men want me, Hamish. I can't help it. God made me that way.

Weed He certainly did that.

Cathleen I made a lot of men happy.

Weed Too many.

Cathleen I never hurt a soul.

Weed reaches across the table, puts his hand on hers.

Weed But it's not a good life is it Cathleen? Not your life. Not my life. Only his. He's dragged us down.

Cathleen You're his lap-dog. That's how he's kept you.

Weed Bastard.

Cathleen I could have been a pure woman.

Weed You were. Once.

Cathleen You could have been a real man.

Weed I was going to be. Once.

Cathleen [*takes her hand from under Weed's*] You know, Hamish, Michael loves us. In his own way he loves the both of us.

Weed You can't help it if a mad dog loves you.

Cathleen He trusts you.

Weed Same difference.

Cathleen Trust isn't easy to come across. Don't scorn it.

Weed It's come too far.

Cathleen [*hides her face in her hands*] Yes. You're right, I think. We have to do it.

Weed It's us or him.

Cathleen Whatever good there is, or was, it's poisoned now.

Over the sounds of the street the clock on the church can be heard sounding.

Weed He's the poison. We have to cut it out. We've got a chance. We won't get another.

Cathleen What if it goes wrong?

Weed Anything can go wrong.

24. Regent's Park

Saturday pm. The Rolls-Royce.

The wind buffets the car. Fairfax examining the gun. Weed looking out at the tennis courts. No-one playing. Weed cheated. Today would have been a good day for women in tennis skirts.

Fairfax Have you touched it?

Weed Is it okay?

Fairfax It's all in order.

Weed I haven't even looked at it.

Fairfax Aren't you curious?

Weed I leave it to you. You know what you're doing.

Fairfax What about Cathleen?

Weed She knows you know what you're doing.

Fairfax Do you?

Weed Do I what?

Fairfax Know what you're doing.

Weed What's this?

Fairfax You seem different today.

Weed You don't trust me? After the trust I've put in you?

Fairfax I didn't say that. I said you seem different. Has something happened, something been changed?

Weed It's all the same as it was.

Fairfax You're sure?

Weed What could change? Everything is going to be the way you wanted it. Slabb wants your bit of paper. He gets it. Big time. You get your snaps.

Fairfax Has he got them ready?

Weed He's sorting it.

Fairfax They're to be in there, in a package on the table, before we go in.

Weed He knows.

Fairfax They'll all be in there?

Weed There's no problem. Slabb never wants to see you again.

Fairfax He's not going to. After tonight. He's not going to be seeing anybody, is he? When's he going to leave them there?

Weed Later on.

Fairfax What time?

Weed Late as possible probably. Kids break in or something.

Fairfax The place has to be locked up before we arrive. I told you that, remember.

Weed It will be. Stop worrying.

Fairfax You're making me worry.

Weed How am I?

Fairfax I don't know. What time are you planting the gun?

Weed Later on. Same reason.

Fairfax Eight o'clock, something like that?

Weed Something like that.

Fairfax On your own?

Weed Of course.

Fairfax Then what, you go back to the flat?

Weed Yeah. Say goodbye to Cathleen.

Fairfax You and Slabb leave from the flat... Cathleen stays there?

Weed There? Can't say. Somewhere. Remember?

Fairfax And Looby Loo?

Weed Meets us at the flat. We all go off together. Why all the questions?

Fairfax I'm the one taking the risks. I'm entitled to ask questions.

Weed It's all sorted. There's no risk.

Fairfax Which is why you won't do it yourself.

Weed We've been through all this.

Fairfax I've got to rely on you, remember.

Weed Well I'm relying on you. So is Cathleen. That's what this is about.

Fairfax Alright.

Weed What time are you getting there?

Fairfax I haven't decided.

Weed Well, don't be late.

Fairfax If I am you'll have to wait, won't you? This is my show.

Weed Okay, okay. How?

Fairfax Cab, I should think.

Weed We'll be parked up outside, waiting.

Fairfax Slabb's pick-up?

Weed It won't be a cab with the meter ticking.

Fairfax There's no need to be like that.

Weed You're asking some odd questions.

Fairfax Something's different.

Weed Nothing's different. Maybe I'm nervous. Of course I'm nervous. There's a lot riding on tonight. The whole rest of my life maybe. Cathleen's life too. That may be nothing to you but it's not nothing to us.

Fairfax You and me both then. We're playing for everything, aren't we?

Weed does not answer, starts to climb out of the Rolls.

...Wish me luck, Weed.

Weed Luck's got nothing to do with it.

25. White City

Saturday pm. The bench by the infants' school.

The school silent for the weekend. The base of the rhododendron bush littered with Friday night's detritus.

Quinn You told Slabb?

Weed Yes.

Quinn What did he say?

Weed He was interested.

Quinn What's he going to do about it?

Weed Didn't say...

Quinn What do you think he'll do?

Weed Make a call, I suppose.

Quinn Where to?

Weed There's a number.

Quinn Ireland?

Weed He doesn't tell me. It changes I think.

Quinn Someone in London?

Weed He gets straight to Ireland. Far as I know.

Quinn He doesn't send word to anyone else?

Weed Such as who?

Quinn I'm asking you.

Weed No.

Quinn Well, okay. You don't tell me everything do you?

Weed Who have you been speaking to?

Quinn No-one.

Weed Cathleen?

Quinn I speak to various people.

Weed What's Cathleen told you?

Quinn Nothing. What is it that she shouldn't have told me?

Weed Nothing.

Quinn At least we understand each other.

Weed You and her? What did she say?

Quinn You and me.

Weed Oh. That's alright.

Quinn How are you about tonight?

Weed Tonight?

Quinn You worried?

Weed Not really... Slightly maybe.

Quinn Big time?

Weed If you want to know.

Quinn I do want to know.

Weed I'm worried. So what?

Quinn Something in particular?

Weed Such as?

Quinn Such as what's going to happen tonight for example.

Weed We know what's going to happen tonight, don't we?

Quinn You might.

Weed Don't you?

Quinn If I knew all the facts you know I might.

Weed You kill me. Big time. What are you on about?

Quinn You tell me.

Weed I'm lost. Jesus.

Quinn Without me you would be. Remember that.

Weed You sound as though you reckon you're about to do me a favour.

Quinn In one.

Weed How?

Quinn I'm going to give you something that may help you out.

Weed What is it?

Quinn A bag of goodies.

Quinn passes Weed a small plastic sandwich bag. Weed opens the bag. Inside are six cartridges.

Weed What are they for?

Quinn Killing people.

Weed What do I do with them?

Quinn Keep them hidden. Don't let Slabb know you've got them.

Weed But what I mean is what do I do with them?

Quinn stands up from the bench.

Quinn That's up to you.

Weed Where are you going?

Quinn My boss. Can't keep him waiting. Know what I mean?

Weed You want to have my boss.

Quinn Weed?

Weed What?

Quinn Tonight's the night.

Weed Yeah, Jesus.

26. White City

Saturday, dusk. Slabb's flat.

Cathleen and Quinn have just finished speaking under the cherry tree in the courtyard of the flats. Quinn has left. Slabb and Weed watching from the balcony as Cathleen climbs the stairs with a shopping bag on each arm. There is something unreal about the sight of her coming in with the weekend provisions at a moment like this. She is moving so slowly that she must have bought in extra for some reason. What is she thinking of?

The two men go inside and wait for her behind the kitchen table. She comes in and heaves the two bags of food onto the table.

> **Slabb** What did he want?
>
> **Cathleen** Quinn?
>
> **Slabb** Father Christmas.
>
> **Cathleen** He told me not to worry. That it would all be over soon.
>
> **Slabb** That's all? It took him a long time to say that.
>
> **Cathleen** Well he's got a way with words, hasn't he? He's a gentleman, by the way.

Cathleen is unloading tin after tin of uncommon delicacies onto the kitchen table. Anchovies, lobster tails, stuffed olives.etc. Slabb stares at the mounting pile of exotic foodstuffs, is for the moment distracted from the critical events shortly to unfold.

Slabb What the hell is this, Christmas again?

Cathleen Well, I thought, why not?

Slabb Why not? How much did that lot cost for Chrissake?

Cathleen We never spoil ourselves. I thought we would. I've got in all your favourites, Michael. And look *[pulling out a huge whole leg of lamb]*, Welsh. And fresh. None of that frozen New Zealand rubbish.

Slabb Am I going to have roast lamb and roast potatoes and then one hour later walk out and have Doctor Fairfax try and shoot me dead? It won't help my digestion.

Weed Sis. I know you mean well. But we're not hungry right now.

Cathleen Not now, stupids. Tomorrow. When it's all over. We'll celebrate with a special dinner.

Slabb Oh yeah? When it's all over, me I'm celebrating with a special drink. You can't beat Sunday lunchtime.

Cathleen And we'll come back and have the lamb. We'll deserve it, after all. Put the kettle on, Michael. I need a cup of tea.

Slabb stands at the sink, fills the kettle. He looks out at the twilight, at the figures merging into shadows. In silence the three actors stand and watch the kettle boil. The tea is made and they sit at the table which is so covered in provisions that they can hardly see each other.

Slabb This is some kind of pantomime. This time you've really gone bananas.

Cathleen *[slaps her forehead]* Bananas. I knew I'd forgotten something. I'll have to go out again.

Weed Bananas. Big time.

Cathleen From now on I'm making a special effort with the dinners. Especially Sundays. You used to love Sunday dinner, Michael.

Slabb I did that.

Cathleen You don't eat properly any more.

Slabb Who's got time to eat? Worries. The business.

Cathleen I'm going to see that you do. One day a week you can forget your worries can't you?

Slabb Sunday morning we'll make love...

Cathleen Are you still up to it?

Slabb You'll soon tell me. After that you'll get up and make breakfast.

Cathleen I'm making the dinner and tidying the house.

Slabb So I'll make breakfast. If I've got any energy left. You'll tidy the house and then we'll go for a walk in the park.

Cathleen The Scrubs? Not that dog toilet at the end of the road.

Slabb Yes. A proper walk. The Scrubs. Or along the canal. Then we'll go to the pub. Early.

Cathleen Church.

Slabb Church? Must we?

Cathleen We must. Everyone else does. Once you've been to church you can do what you want. You'll have to put a suit on.

Slabb I've still got one, haven't I?

Weed I haven't.

Slabb You don't have to come.

Weed I can't walk all along the canal or round the bloody Scrubs. You know that. What with my leg.

Slabb You don't have to come.

Weed And I don't drink either.

Slabb There's no law says you have to go to the pub.

Weed Well what will I do?

Slabb You can do what you want.

Weed Suppose I want to be with you, or my sister?

Slabb I'm just saying there's no law says you have to do what we do.

Cathleen When was the last time we had a holiday together?

Weed Never.

Cathleen We could take a few days, couldn't we?

Slabb Somewhere we've never been?

Weed We've never been anywhere. We just said that.

Cathleen The Lakes?

Slabb Abroad?

Weed Abroad? No. Too hot.

Cathleen I don't like it too hot.

Slabb I don't like it hot at all.

Cathleen The Lakes then?

Weed What do you do at the Lakes, walk a lot?

Cathleen When?

Slabb Next week?

Weed Suppose Brady's here?

Slabb He isn't going to be is he?

Weed Well, suppose he is.

Slabb What if he is?

Weed He won't take kindly to you walking off on holiday.

Slabb Why not?

Weed He'll take it personal.

Cathleen Too bad.

Weed You're going to tell Brady 'too bad'?

Slabb I'll tell him.

Cathleen I don't care if he does come. He had his chance with me years ago.

Slabb You look after him, Weed. Show him the place, the business.

Weed He's not coming.

Cathleen For all I care he can have the business. Who needs it?

Slabb Ah, well. We all need it.

Cathleen Why do we?

Slabb What would we do without it?

Cathleen We'd be free maybe.

Slabb Free to do what? Some different business?

Cathleen Free to be.

Slabb Free to be pushed around.

Cathleen We're pushed around anyway. By the business. We didn't choose that.

Slabb There are no choices, Cathleen. No real ones. The only choices we get to make are ones that make no difference.

Cathleen Some people have choices.

Slabb Not us.

Cathleen So there's nothing we can do?

Slabb We can dream. No one can stop us doing that.

Cathleen Only us. We stop ourselves.

Slabb Perhaps we do.

Weed Brady's not going to come. We've seen to that.

Slabb We've all seen to a lot of things. All we can do is do what we do and hope to get lucky. Do you feel lucky, Weed?

Weed Lucky? Me?

Slabb You. Do you feel lucky tonight?

Weed I never feel lucky.

Slabb That's what I thought. We're none of us lucky, are we?

Cathleen We will be. One day.

Weed It's getting on. I'd better be going. Where's the bag with the gun?

Cathleen On the bed.

Weed fetches the Woolworth bag, brings it into the kitchen.

Slabb Is it loaded?

Weed With the dummies. I had to put the live bullets back in to show The Doc this afternoon. I swapped them over again.

Slabb Let's see.

Slabb takes the bag from Weed, opens the cylinder and empties the dummy rounds onto the table]

    Slabb [continued] OK. Load it up again.

Weed reloads the dummies, closes the cylinder.

    Slabb [continued] Where are the live bullets?
    Weed In the bedroom.
    Slabb Fetch them.
    Weed Why?
    Slabb Fetch them.

Weed fetches the red cardboard box that holds the ten live cartridges. He gives it to Slabb.

    Weed What are you going to do with them?

Slabb takes the box from Weed and puts it in his pocket.

    Slabb Keep them... Well, what are you waiting for? You've got to go and plant the gun, haven't you?

Weed picks up the Woolworth bag and leaves. The front door slams. Weed's footsteps on the stone stairs.

    Cathleen My bananas. I've got to catch the shop.
    Slabb Shall I come with you?
    Cathleen For some bananas? Are you going soft?

27. Sands End

Saturday, 7.45 pm. Helen's flat.

The street door to the house where Helen Suter lives is ajar. Quinn pushes it open and steps into the hallway of the house, listens for sounds from upstairs. There are none. At the foot of the stairs he stops and listens again. He calls her name.

On the first floor the door to the flat is open. There is still no sound from inside. Calling out again he walks through to the bedroom.

She is lying fully clothed on her back on the bed. She is dead. Her blue eyes staring up at the ceiling as if she has can see heaven. Her white freckled face wrapped in the carroty mop of her hair.

Quinn guesses that she has overdosed. She could have held her own in a fight against most men but the room shows no sign of a struggle. It seems exactly as it was when he left her thirty six hours before. Could she have had a heart attack, or a stroke? The way she treated herself, she had it coming. At least she seems to have died in her sleep. She is wearing her leather suit and like the good trooper that she was she has died with her boots on. But she is not wearing the leather belt.

Quinn searches the bedroom for the belt but cannot find it. He looks in the bedding, under the bed, in cupboards and drawers, anywhere that clothes might be kept. It is not in the bathroom. On the draining board in the kitchen he finds the belt and beside it a sharp kitchen knife. The bronze snake's head buckle has been cut off.

Quinn goes back to the bedroom. He stands over her as he did before, looks down at her face. Perhaps she has found peace, finally got where she was always going. He sinks into the battered armchair facing the end of the bed, stares at the scene.

Later, he tries to make a call from Helen's phone. The line is dead. He stops the Ford by a call box.

28. White City

Saturday 8pm. The Crypt.

Cathleen catches Weed as he is unlocking the steel mesh outer door of the club.

Weed Sis, what are you doing here?

Cathleen I wanted to check you're alright.

Weed I don't need checking on. I'm not a kid.

Cathleen *[pointing at his back]* Look at you. You've gone and got bird's muck on your jacket. How did you manage that?

Weed It was easy. *[Unlocks inner steel door]*

Cathleen It's a good luck sign, you know.

Weed I never have good luck. Ever.

Cathleen Well maybe tonight you will.

Weed Are you coming in?

Cathleen I better.

Weed What about Michael?

Cathleen Thinks I've gone for bananas. I'll tell him I couldn't find any.

They go in. Slabb's drinking club is a bare walled, concrete floored rectangle-it can hardly be called a room- that must have been built as a small workshop. In one corner a smaller closed off rectangle, a service area of washroom and toilets, feeds off the main one. There are no windows. In the main room the only daylight would come from narrow 'lights' set in the walls just beneath the ceiling. In the service area obscure glass skylights are set into the roof. One over the toilet cubicles and a larger one over the sink. In the main room powerful striplights are mounted in the ceiling. These are on now. A cctv monitor is fixed above the door. It shows the scene, pavement and roadway, outside the front door.

Cheap table lamps provide the 'ambience' when the club is in use. Armchairs and sofas rescued from the authority tip are scattered between a selection of pub tables, garden tables and even two school desks. In one corner there is a municipal park bench, courtesy, somehow, of Liverpool City Council and dedicated to the memory of one Eileen Ross 'who loved this spot'. Another corner of the room is the bar area. Wall mounted shelves are stacked with beer, wine, liquor and glasses. Under the shelves is a small fridge.

Cathleen helps Weed arrange the room. They leave the largest pub table in a cleared space in the centre of the room with two chairs on either side.

Cathleen The gun?

Weed The gun.

Cathleen You're going to do it?

Weed It's decided.

Cathleen It is.

Weed I will then. You keep watch.

Cathleen What for?

Weed Anybody coming.

Cathleen Nobody's coming.

Weed Keep watch anyway.

Weed goes into the back washroom. Here there is

nothing but a sink with a cupboard under it. At the end of this section a partitioned off area has two toilet cubicles. Weed puts the Woolworth bag on the sink draining board and takes out the Colt. He thumbs the cylinder catch, pushes out the cylinder and empties the dummy rounds onto the draining board. From his jacket pocket he takes out the sandwich bag that Quinn gave him and from it loads a live cartridge into one of the chambers. He picks up a second cartridge and is about to load it when he stops what he is doing...

He returns the cartridge he is holding to the bag then empties the live cartridge from the chamber and puts it back with the others. He puts the sandwich bag back in his pocket. He reloads the dummy rounds, closes the cylinder, puts the gun in the Woolworth bag and replaces it in the cupboard under the sink. He goes back to the bar.

Cathleen You did it?

Weed Of course.

Cathleen Did it go alright?

Weed There's nothing to go wrong is there? You could do it yourself.

Cathleen I've seen you do it enough times... You don't look well, you know.

Weed I don't feel it.

Cathleen What?

Weed My gut.

Cathleen You'd better go to the toilet, hadn't you?

Weed Now?

Cathleen You might not get another chance.

Weed You're right. I need a crap.

Cathleen Go on then. Give me your jacket first.

Weed Why?

Cathleen You can't walk around with bird's muck on your back. People won't take you seriously. I'll wash it off while you're in there.

Weed takes off his jacket, hands it to Cathleen without looking at it.

Weed Thanks, sis. You think of everything.

Weed goes through to the toilets. He slams the door of a cubicle. He can be heard groaning. Cathleen takes Weed's jacket to the sink and turns the tap on full. The noise of the water hitting the metal sink drowns out the noise of Weed shitting.

29. White City

Saturday 9.45pm. The Crypt.
Outside, Slabb and Weed wait in a Ford Pick Up. Inside, Quinn waits in the washroom, the skylight open.

At two minutes to ten a London cab pulls up behind Slabb's Pick Up. Alec Fairfax pays off the driver.

Slabb gets out of the Pick Up, goes to stand in front of the unmarked and unsigned door of the club. Weed remains in the Pick Up. Fairfax stares into the Pick Up then walks across to join Slabb. The two men acknowledge each other.

On a sign from Slabb Fairfax assumes the position. Slabb frisks him. He is clean. Slabb assumes the position. Fairfax finds him clean, then turns towards the Pick Up.

Fairfax I see Weed. I don't see Looby Loo.

Slabb You wouldn't, would you?

Fairfax She had to be here.

Slabb She couldn't make it.

Fairfax Where is she?

Slabb In the mortuary.

Fairfax She's dead? How?

Slabb OD'd probably. Died last night or this morning. We thought you might have known.

Fairfax How do you know this?

Slabb We sent a cab for her. He came back with the story. He got it off the copper guarding her door.

Fairfax The police? You said she overdosed.

Slabb Probably overdosed they said.

Fairfax How do I know this is true?

Slabb That's for you to say.

Fairfax What is that supposed to mean?

Slabb You tell me.

Fairfax You could have sent word.

Slabb We thought you might call it off. We didn't want that.

Fairfax You seem to think I had a hand in it.

Slabb Easy enough for a doctor. Inject her with something. Her arms were like pin cushions anyway.

Fairfax What do you want to do?

Slabb What do you want to do?

Fairfax What I came here to do.

Slabb Let's do it then.

Slabb unlocks the outer and inner doors, walks in and turns on the lights. Fairfax follows him in. The room is as Weed and Cathleen left it. One table in the centre of the room with two chairs. On the table a manilla business envelope, size A4.

Slabb *[gestures at the envelope]* Your snaps, Doc. Feel free to look around. If you're worried.

Fairfax looks around the room. It is obviously empty apart from them. He and Slabb go through to the washroom area. He sees this too is empty. He looks into the toilet cubicles.

Fairfax Show me the photos.

They go back to the main room and sit at the table facing each other. Slabb pushes the envelope to Fairfax who opens it and begins examining the contents, a pile of 7x9 prints and several strips of negatives.

Fairfax Harmless fun?

Slabb Nothing personal.

Fairfax So I've been told.

Slabb You were careless.

Fairfax Unlucky, I would have said. Is this all of them?

Slabb Check the negs.

Fairfax holds film up to the light, checks each frame.

Fairfax There could be copies. Of the prints or the negatives.

Slabb There aren't.

Fairfax How do I know there aren't other films?

Slabb You have to trust me.

Fairfax replaces prints and negatives into envelope.

Fairfax Unfortunately, I do have to trust you. Okay, get Weed in. Let's do this.

Slabb goes to door, signals to Pick-up. In a moment Weed enters room, closes door behind him. Slabb indicates wall mounted phone.

Slabb Time to make that call, Doc.

Fairfax *[dials and connects]* This is Doctor Fairfax, you're expecting my call? Your rider can now make the delivery to the address I specified. Five minutes? He knows what to do?... Yes, to me only... *[To Slabb]* You got all that?

Slabb You know what was agreed. Weed takes the photos and stands outside till I call him back in.

Fairfax It's hardly necessary.

Slabb It is to me.

Weed picks up envelope and goes back outside.

Fairfax Look, Slabb. I don't feel too good. Could I get a drink while we wait?

Slabb Help yourself.

Fairfax Can you make me a gin and tonic?

Slabb Make you a drink?

Fairfax It's your bar.

Slabb Are you paying?

Fairfax I've got to take a leak.

Slabb Nervous, eh?

Fairfax Frankly.

Slabb Ice and lemon, Doctor?

Slabb goes behind bar while Fairfax walks through to washroom area. From main room Fairfax can be heard closing one of cubicle doors. There is no sound of him urinating before, shortly, toilet is flushed. Sound of water running from the tap over metal sink.

Washroom.

Tap running. Fairfax opens cupboard under sink. The Woolworth bag is there. He takes Colt out of bag and with hands still inside cupboard he opens cylinder and checks that it is loaded. He closes cylinder, puts gun in pocket of his coat. He turns off tap and goes back to main room. Slabb is sitting at the table with two gin and tonics prepared. Fairfax sits down.

>**Slabb** Couldn't go?
>
>**Fairfax** No.
>
>**Slabb** *[raising his glass]* Cheers, Doc.

Fairfax raises his glass to Slabb.

>**Fairfax** Let this be an end of it.

Outside, the sound of a motorbike. Both men look up at the cctv screen on the wall. They see a helmeted rider getting off a motorbike, propping it on its side stand. Weed watching him. The rider adjusts the shoulder sac on his back then bends to takes a bulky package from the bike sidebox. Weed and the rider exchange words. The rider seems to know what is expected of him and he opens the package and gives it to Weed. Weed can be seen pulling a plastic bound document from the package, glancing at it and then putting it back in the package.

Inside. Washroom. From the roof Quinn lifts the skylight open, looks through then lowers himself down until his feet touch the sink draining board. He pulls the skylight to, climbs down and goes into one of the toilet cubicles.

Inside. Main room. The door opens.

Weed It's here.

Slabb Show him in.

Courier walks in. Weed goes back outside, as agreed.

Courier *[talks through visor of helmet]* Doctor Fairfax?

Fairfax That's me.

Courier Your delivery. *[hands package to Fairfax]*

Fairfax Thank you. Could you wait over there for a minute? There'll be something to go back.

Courier stands to one side. Fairfax turns to Slabb.

...Your merchandise. Check it through.

Slabb pulls out document, begins to 'read' it, or anyway look at it. He flips through top few pages running his index finger under various words. The top page of the document reads 'MEDICAL REPORT' - 'prepared by DR. ARMAND DRIVER FRCPsych'. The second page is headed 'Resume of findings of psychiatric tests conducted on MR STEPHEN SIMPSON. List of tests and investigations carried out with the consent of the patient'

Slabb *[recognising Secretary's name]* SIMPSON. That's him...

Fairfax *[indicating courier with his eyes]* Don't say any more... Satisfied?

Slabb This'll do.

Fairfax Can I have my package now?

Slabb Call Weed in.

Fairfax *[to courier]* Would you mind asking the man outside to come in?

Courier goes to door, lets Weed in, closes door.

...I want you to take this package to the address that your controller has been given. You know about this?

Fairfax takes package of photos from Weed, seals it and hands it to courier. Courier turns to leave, reaches door then stops and turns back. Slabb, Weed and Fairfax look at him.

Courier Sorry. Forgot to get you to sign for the delivery.

Courier comes back, stands over the table. He reaches into his shoulder sac, takes out a snub nosed revolver and without a word shoots Slabb dead with a single shot to the head. Fairfax, who has had his hand on the Colt in his pocket, stands up and automatically pulls it out without aiming it in any particular direction. Courier takes Fairfax with a second clean shot to the head. Fairfax drops the Colt, falls over the table, dead.

Quinn runs into the room, stops by Fairfax's body as he sees what has happened.

Courier Quinn. Get on the floor. Lie down.

Quinn lies down beside Fairfax' body.

Weed Donal! You're here already? It's me, Weed! You remember me, Cathleen's brother. Thank God you've come. She's waiting for you now, back at the flat. We thought you were coming tomorrow.

Courier raises his revolver, takes aim at Weed's heart.

Weed Donal! It's me, Hamish! You recognise me. Don't shoot. Jesus, don't shoot!

Courier shoots Weed twice in the chest, walks across to Weed's body, checks he is dead. Goes back to the table, picks up medical report, puts it into his shoulder sac. Doing this he watches, amused, as Quinn snatches up the Colt and trains it on him.

Courier I've read the plot too, Quinn... Rest in peace.

Quinn fires three times, killing the courier with two shots to the heart, one to the throat.

He kneels over the courier, pulls off his helmet, looks into the face of Trafalgar's driver. He looks down at the man's hand, pulls the snake's head ring from his finger. He goes to pick up the driver's revolver but then withdraws his hand without touching it. He picks up the shoulder sac that holds the report as well as Fairfax's photos.

Outside The Crypt he walks quickly through a small group of people who have gathered by the door on hearing the shots.

30. White City

Epilogue
Sunday pm. The empty church.

Quinn and Cathleen in the front pew. The bleeding Christ looking down on them.

Cathleen He came for me. I prayed for him to come and he came bringing death and destruction.

Quinn Brady was no saviour. He killed Michael, Weed and Doctor Fairfax.

Cathleen At my bidding. My sins have brought this to pass. Now I'm left alone to contemplate them... I don't have the strength to take my own life. He knows that.

Quinn Your sins?

Cathleen It was me switched the bullets for the dummies.

Quinn You were bound to. You and your brother had made a pact. Weed was always going to chicken out at the death. Isn't that just what I said to you under the cherry tree?

Cathleen You used me.

Quinn I had to. Everyone who knew about the blackmail was going to be there in the same place at the same time.

Cathleen Not your boss.

Quinn Not him.

Cathleen Helen.

Quinn She was dead anyway.

Cathleen Not me.

Quinn We all had to die. The Doctor. Michael. Weed. Me. You too, if you'd been there.

Cathleen Then I should have been there. It would be better. I made a mistake.

Quinn I don't call saving my life a mistake.

Cathleen I should have died there.

Quinn You knew Weed was weak. What you did, you did for him. Because he wanted it.

Cathleen I wanted it myself. I can't pretend. It was my hand that loaded the gun.

Quinn Your hand had nothing to do with the deaths of Michael and Weed. That was Brady's doing.

Cathleen He was carrying out my wishes.

Quinn He didn't know your wishes.

Cathleen He knows everything.

Quinn Brady's dead.

Cathleen By my hand.

Quinn No. By mine.

Cathleen I've killed my own saviour.

Quinn He was a man. No more.

Cathleen He came for me. That much I know.

Quinn He did. They can't take that from you.

Cathleen Would he have kept me?

Quinn He came for you didn't he?

Cathleen Sent to punish me perhaps.

Quinn It's me that has punished you.

Cathleen You did what you had to. Is one life worth more than another?

Quinn When it's your own.

Cathleen Was I wrong to want Michael gone? I didn't want him dead. I just wanted him gone.

Quinn Weed wanted him dead. He wanted blood. What you did you did for him.

Cathleen Hamish couldn't stand to see me badly treated.

Quinn What he couldn't stand was that he was too weak to do anything about it...

PAUSE

Cathleen The Secretary...

Quinn A story. Trafalgar gave it to the papers.

Cathleen Michael working for him, this Trafalgar?

Quinn Part of the story.

Cathleen That much couldn't be true. Not Michael..Another one of his lies?

Quinn Michael's, or Trafalgar's?

Cathleen Does it matter?... Would the doctor have killed Michael?

Quinn I doubt it.

Cathleen Alec Fairfax was a big softy.....So what was he going to do?

Quinn I don't think he knew himself. Did he even believe Weed's story?

Cathleen Weed wasn't sure.

Quinn Weed was more frightened of Michael finding out than he was of being stuck with him for life.

Cathleen My brother was a coward. It's true. It's not a sin... Trafalgar will come for me then?

Quinn You can't harm him.

Cathleen He can come. Any time. The sooner the better.

Quinn Don't speak like that.

Cathleen I'm ready... But you?

Quinn I'm dead already.

PAUSE

Cathleen Michael loved me you know.

Quinn I do know.

Cathleen They loved me... They're dead... What does that mean?

Quinn Others will love you. If you let them.

Cathleen How could I? When loving me brings about a man's death. I told you before I make wrong choices. Punished, for choosing wrong.

Quinn The punishment is harsh.

Cathleen It would have been so easy to choose right. What stopped me?

Quinn Would it have been right, with Brady?

Cathleen I make wrong choices.

Quinn The punishment is cruel.

Cathleen It is. I made a wrong choice. Nothing changes that. What am I to do, Quinn?

Quinn Build a new life.

Cathleen When I make wrong choices?

Quinn Make them anyway. Someone will love you.

Cathleen They all loved me...

Quinn Cathleen...

Cathleen I told you I'd have to burn. Wrong choices. It's my lot... Wrong choices...

Quinn leaves her talking to the figure of Christ. The church is still empty.

31. Ireland

Epilogue
Driving rain. A distant view of cliffs, windswept moorland...
A lonely graveyard beside a ruined stone church.

The motorbike with the 'ZZ DISPATCH' insignia pulls off the road and through the broken graveyard gates. The rider stops the machine beside a stone slab that marks the top of a grave, kills both the motor and the lights. He takes the key out of the ignition. The pillion passenger, who has the hood of his oilskins up, gets off as does the rider. The rider lifts his visor. 'Got to take a leak.'

The passenger grunts from inside his hood.

The rider, not turning his back on the man in oilskins, stands up in front of an oak tree. His piss steams on the damp ground. He zips up and returns to passenger.

Rider Want a drink?

Passenger What?

Rider A drink?

Passenger [laughs inside hood] Well, what have you got, whisky?

Rider [laughs with passenger] Exactly. In the side box. And it's Irish.

Passenger Fuck sake, get it out!

The rider kneels by the bike, opens the side box. He takes out a bottle of Jameson and lobs it to the passenger.

The passenger catches it with both hands, pulls the cork and begins tipping the drink down his throat.

The rider reaches into the side box again and, in one movement, takes out a long barrelled Smith and Wesson 44 Magnum. From the kneeling position he fires three shots into the heart of his passenger. He stands up and calmly checks his work, uprights the fallen whiskey bottle, then puts the gun away in the side box before dragging the body to the stone slab beside the bike. The slab, which has been prepared, slides easily on wooden runners to reveal an open empty coffin. The rider manhandles the body into the coffin and closes the lid. He slides the slab back into place, pulls out the runners and the slab drops two inches into its slot in the ground. He retrieves whiskey bottle and, standing over the grave, toasts the passenger and crosses himself mockingly.

Cliffs overlooking a windswept coast.

On the clifftop the ZZ -DISPATCH motorbike is on its side stand, the rider standing beside it. He turns the key in the ignition, pushes the bike off its stand, puts it in gear and aims it over the cliff. The rider takes off his gloves and then his helmet. We do not see his face but see the bronze snake's head ring on his finger. He throws the helmet and gloves after the bike.

Pan to view of distant headland, the open sea.

32. London Street

Epilogue
Monday pm. A new week begins. Across from the dead gardens, Trafalgar's Jaguar.

It is a sunny day. On the bench, alone, the woman wino with the good legs. Red faced in the sun, she is drinking from a can of strong beer. Her short skirt is up.

On the back seat between Quinn and Trafalgar the package containing Fairfax's photos as well as 'the report on The Secretary'.

Quinn looks towards the dead gardens. On the bench the woman is swinging one of her legs, holding out an unlit cigarette and smiling at passing office men. Quinn takes the report out of the envelope and flips the pages.

Quinn New driver?

Trafalgar I'll keep that.

Quinn Cover and opening pages typed by Fairfax. Enough to fool Slabb who could barely read. The rest photocopied pages from some medical journal.

Trafalgar Paddington and King's Cross. Where worlds meet.

Quinn King's Cross. You stumbled on an upmarket doctor with a downmarket habit. You and the Marquis were in business. Then the doctor started to unwind your knitting... You sleep with the enemy?

Trafalgar Sometimes your enemy wants the same things as you... You left the gun.

Quinn The gun that Brady, or your chauffeur, used on those guards? It had to be... .38 Special. Probably it also killed Brady himself. I don't know.

Trafalgar The Colt?

Quinn Cathleen's prints. My own.

Trafalgar This changes nothing.

Quinn It was meant to change everything. The government of the country. My own existence.

Trafalgar To a man in your position, Quinn, all that is nothing.

Quinn gets out of the car. Across the street the woman on the bench is still swinging her leg, still looking for a light.

Quinn stands in the street, lets the traffic and dust go past him. He takes the air in deep. London Street smells the same as ever. That mix of things fresh and rotten, old and new. London Street will go on smelling. The sun will go on shining. Quinn crosses the street.

* * *

Rights Enquiries

Rights and permission enquires can be made via email to the author at:

penrhyschristian@gmail.com

Printed in Great Britain
by Amazon.co.uk, Ltd.,
Marston Gate.